CW01096040

Putting Daoist Thought into Practice

This book shows how Chinese wisdom originating many centuries ago is still highly relevant to our lives today as the Daoist classics provide insightful prescriptions on how to live a life full of happiness, contentment, and healthy longevity. They also provide guidance regarding personal ethics, sustainable economics, and achieving enlightenment.

The book contains reflections on how to achieve happiness drawing from the *Liezi*, a Daoist classic, and it examines Daoist ideas about nourishing life to achieve longevity and the marked similarity between these principles and people living in "blue zones" today with the highest concentration of centenarians. It explores Daoist views on consciousness and enlightenment in the *Laozi* and *Zhuangzi* and their close resemblance to some of the most influential "new age" teachings on the subject. It highlights the ethical character of a Daoist sage by drawing on the Daoist classic of the *Wenzi* and enumerates lessons for transitioning toward a sustainable economy from the *Daodejing*.

Covering multiple dimensions of classical Daoist thought and their contemporary applications to human development and well-being, this text will usefully inform scholars, students, and researchers of Asian studies, religion, and philosophy, and individuals seeking self-improvement and personal wellness.

Devin K. Joshi is an Associate Professor in the School of Social Sciences at Singapore Management University.

To Leigh,
Wishing you all the
best!

"Devin Joshi's new work places ancient Daoist ideals and teachings into a dialogue with modern values and issues, focusing on the pursuit of happiness, the quest for longevity, the yearning for inner peace, the ethics of leadership, and the sustainability of the environment. In each of the five chapters, he presents a comprehensive and coherent outline of the Daoist vision, based on key classics that include but also go beyond the central works of Laozi and Zhuangzi, then matches this with contemporary theories and studies, such as the blue zones of centenarian living and Eckhart Tolle's concept of Being. The book, well organized and easy to read, makes an important contribution to the contemporary relevance and adaption of ancient Chinese wisdom. It is inspiring for those interested in Daoism and Chinese thought but an absolute must for anyone interested in ways of creating a more harmonious and more sustainable world."

Livia Kohn, *Professor, Boston University*, United States

"*Putting Daoist Thought into Practice* is a scholarly and timely book that engagingly explores the contemporary and timeless themes of happiness, longevity and human potential, whilst also considering the ways Daoist teachings may guide us towards more ethical and sustainable ways of living. Professor Devin K. Joshi convincingly demonstrates how ancient wisdom can meaningfully inform, and potentially transform, modern times."

Elliot Cohen, *Chartered Psychologist, Chair of the British Psychological Society's Transpersonal Psychology Section, Senior Lecturer in Social Psychology and Interdisciplinary Psychology at Leeds Beckett University*, United Kingdom

Putting Daoist Thought into Practice

Happiness, Longevity, and Enlightenment

Devin K. Joshi

Routledge
Taylor & Francis Group

LONDON AND NEW YORK

First published 2025
by Routledge
4 Park Square, Milton Park, Abingdon, Oxon, OX14 4RN

and by Routledge
605 Third Avenue, New York, NY 10158

Routledge is an imprint of the Taylor & Francis Group, an informa business

British Library Cataloguing-in-Publication Data
A catalogue record for this book is available from the British Library

ISBN: 9781032852560 (hbk)
ISBN: 9781032852591 (pbk)
ISBN: 9781003517344 (ebk)

DOI: 10.4324/9781003517344

Typeset in Times New Roman
by KnowledgeWorks Global Ltd.

Contents

Acknowledgments

Many people have played an important role in making this book possible. I would like to thank Clarissa Lim at Routledge for her keen interest and support of this project. I am deeply grateful to the book's anonymous reviewers for providing great suggestions on how to improve the manuscript. Various scholars have shaped and inspired my thinking about Daoism over the years. As a student, my earliest mentors in the study of Daoism were Poul Anderson, Florian C. Reiter, and Fabrizio Pregadio. I have also benefitted from having many excellent teachers of the Chinese language over the years starting with Drs. Hong Zeng and Wendy Abraham when I was an undergraduate student at Stanford University. Later on in my career since joining the faculty of Singapore Management University (SMU), I have been very fortunate to exchange ideas about Daoism and related subjects with a number of colleagues. Steven Burik has greatly helped me to understand Daoist thinking from a philosophical and comparative perspective. Ijlal Naqvi graciously motivated me to pursue my studies of Daoism at a time when I had developed a renewed interest in the subject. On the interrelationship between Daoist thought and happiness, I learned much from conversations with Matthew Hammerton and Andree Hartanto. I have also been well supported to conduct the research for this book by Chandran Kukathas, Dean of the School of Social Sciences at SMU, and I am grateful for receiving a Lee Kong Chian Fellowship from SMU and a sabbatical leave to help me complete this project.

Outside of Singapore, I would like to especially thank Livia Kohn from whom I have learned very much and whose deep knowledge about Daoism has been a constant source of inspiration to me. The first chapter of this book (on happiness) is based on a paper presented at the 16th International Conference on Daoist Studies at Leeds Beckett University in June 2023. I am grateful to Elliot Cohen, Lea Cantor, Steve Geisz, Marnix Wells, David Chai, and other participants at that conference for valuable suggestions and comments on that paper. The fourth chapter of this book (on ethics) is based on a paper presented at the 17th International Conference on Daoist Studies held in Taichung, Taiwan, in January 2024. I thank Livia Kohn and Fiona Hsin-Fang Chang for organizing that conference where I learned a lot from the many participants. I am grateful for valuable suggestions and comments I received on that paper from Erik Hoogcarspel, Daniel Paracka, Terry Kleeman, Bernadette Rigard-Cellard, Michael Wesch, and J. Gordon Melton. I would also like to thank my former colleague Gao Yang for introducing me to the Blue Zones which ended up fascinating me and led to the writing of the second chapter of this book about longevity.

I am grateful for being able to reuse two previous publications in this book. Chapter 1 first appeared in Devin Joshi. 2024. "An Integrated Theory of Happiness: The Yang Zhu Chapter of the *Liezi*." *Journal of Daoist Studies* 17(1): 1–25. Chapter 2 previously appeared in Devin Joshi. 2021. "The Way of Longevity: Blue Zones as Unselfconscious Models of Daoist Living." *Journal of Daoist Studies* 14(1): 128–151. Those chapters reappear here with some modifications thanks to the kind permission of the editors of the *Journal of Daoist Studies*.

I conclude by expressing my indescribable appreciation for the endless love and support I have received from my wife Hyun Joo and daughter Lina and also for the kind and caring long-term support I have received from my loving mother and parents-in-law. I would also like to express immense gratitude to close friends and family members for encouraging me to engage in this project and for supporting me in other ways. I dedicate this book to my late father whom I miss very much.

Preface

Welcome to a book that may change your life. At first glance, Daoist thought may seem confusing and difficult to put into practice. This challenge was foreseen thousands of years ago by the author(s) of the most influential book in the Daoist tradition, the *Daodejing* (a.k.a. *Tao Te Ching*), often translated as the "Classic of the Way and Its Virtue." That text is a legendary anthology accredited to the Daoist sage Laozi (a.k.a. Lao-tzu) whose moniker means the "Old Master." The *Daodejing* (DDJ) tells us that the *Dao* (a.k.a. *Tao*) often translated as "the Way" cannot be fully understood or communicated via language. As the opening lines of the DDJ relate, "The Way that can be told of is not the eternal Way. Names that can be named are not constant names." The stanza conveys that we humans are too finite and weak to fully understand the great mysteries of the universe including "the Way," the generative source of everything in the cosmos. Even what we think we know is true in this world is difficult to pass on to others because human language is ambiguous and always changing. Therefore, as humans, we should be humble at all times and recognize that true knowledge is not easily accessible.

In the Daoist tradition, the elusive, obscure, and ineffable yet omnipresent great *Dao* (道) or "Way" is viewed as the source of all life and creativity in the cosmos. By implication, things go best when leaders on Earth follow this cosmic "Way." As Wang (2012: 46, 58) explains,

> The *Dao* is the unitary source of heaven, earth, and human beings, and it is the model or pattern they all follow (*Daodejing* 25). *Dao* becomes the source of all existence such that there is nothing beyond the *Dao*. Although there are many different interpretations of the meaning of *Dao* in the *Daodejing*, *Dao* is generally taken as the ultimate origin, source, and principle of the universe and the myriad things... A young girl becoming a mother is the way of the *Dao*; Laozi's *Dao* is the mother of all myriad things. Another important point is that, as the soil to a seed, the mother provides a nourishing condition that allows things to grow and flourish, just as the female body supplies all nutrients for a

foetus to survive and develop. This appreciation is different than simply one event of creation.

At the same time, Daos or "ways" of success may be particular to a specific domain in life (e.g. Hansen 1992; Phan 2007), and there are multiple meanings for the polysemic concept of *Dao* (e.g. Coutinho 2014: 23–26). As Sterckx (2019: 73–74) explains,

> Chinese thinkers propose multiple '*Daos*' or methods, each providing different answers to the 'how' question…as a concept *Dao* is elastic. Its meaning stretches from describing the underlying pattern that governs the universe to the way people should live their lives and, in a narrower sense, a method: the way of warfare, the way of the sage, the way of the gentleman, the way of the ancients, the way of governing, the way of the body."

Despite these challenges, the elusive nature of the Way and the fundamental indeterminacies of human language have not repelled many people who, for thousands of years, have found themselves deeply attracted to the sagely teachings of the Daoist tradition.

The Way continues to be attractive to people living in the modern world today because learning about the Way and incorporating awareness of the Way into our lives can potentially bring about a fundamental transformation in ourselves and the world for the better. In the 21st century, many people are looking for solutions to address the crises we face of unchecked greed and modern life stress while yearning for health, happiness, and a new level of consciousness. Some even fear that our world is entering a civilizational dead-end grounded in capitalism and modernity. In response to these concerns, the timeless wisdom of Daoist teachings provides sorely needed guidance for improving human happiness and achieving a more harmonious society.

The aim of this book is to bring audiences to the living wisdom of Daoism in daily life. It focuses on general applications of Daoist thought to anyone, anywhere in the world. Instead of treating Daoist thought as something abstract, technical, ancient, or foreign, this book exposes how core ideas in Daoism can be and have already been implemented in the world through practical applications ranging from ethics and economics to the attainment of longevity, happiness, and enlightenment. Beginning at the individual level and extending outward to the societal and global context, this book is an illustration of how Daoist principles and ideas can and do live and breathe in the world today. As the book demonstrates, many people applying Daoistic principles to astonishing effect have paradoxically never even heard of Daoism – not just fictional characters like Winnie the Pooh – but also real-life people like you and me.

In that sense, this book is not alone in offering Daoist insights on how to improve our lives. Over the past half century, an influential author to make Daoist thinking accessible to Western audiences was Alan Watts who wrote many books on the subject including *Tao: The Watercourse Way* (Watts 1975). Several years later, Hoff (2009/1982) wrote about how a certain fictional character mentioned in the paragraph above embodied key Daoist principles of naturalness and uncontrived simplicity. Drawing from a wealth of classical Daoist texts, Livia Kohn has also written much over the years about how Daoist practices can enrich our lives and longevity through modifications in diet, exercise, meditation, and so on (e.g. Kohn 2010). Slingerland (2014) has written in *Trying Not to Try* about how following our intuition often reflects the Daoist principle of effortless, non-calculative action. Coutinho (2014) explains some of the key ideas and differences among early Daoist thinkers. And more recently, Culham and Lin (2020) have enumerated the value of fostering healthy *qi* (bioenergetic potency) and virtue to live a good life. These works are of great value, and I encourage interested readers to learn from these and other readings to go beyond what is covered in this book.

What this book offers is a unique and comparative perspective on several dimensions of Daoist thought. Books about Daoism tend to fall into one of five categories. Firstly, there are books about Daoism as a *religion*. Often written by self-identified Daoists in or from East Asia or by scholars who have spent months or years at Daoist temples or monasteries, these books chronicle the rituals and lives of modern Daoist priests, nuns, practitioners, and temple communities. Secondly, there are *historical* books about Daoist communities or individuals living in China (or elsewhere in Asia) generations ago based on the analysis of old texts. Thirdly, there are books written about Daoist *philosophy* that tend to approach the subject from a relatively abstract, logical, critical, or technical angle and are often difficult to understand for the average reader. Those books tend to pay little attention to (or are outright dismissive of) historical Daoist communities or the practice of Daoist religion in historical or contemporary times. Fourthly, there are books which look more specifically at applications of Daoist ideas and practices within a *single domain* in areas such as *fengshui*, *qigong*, architecture, diet, exercise, meditation, sex, longevity, etc. Fifthly, there are books which provide *translations* or commentaries on specific classical Daoist texts. To the person able and willing to read some (or all) of these five different types of books, much knowledge and wisdom can be acquired.

This book does not fall into any of those five categories. It is neither about history nor organized religion. It does not engage in abstract and technical philosophical discussions. Nor does it provide a new translation or commentary on a classical scripture. Rather, it is a book of original scholarship that analyzes portions of several influential classical Daoist texts (namely *Laozi*, *Wenzi*, *Liezi*, *Zhuangzi*, and texts from the *Yangsheng* tradition) to provide insights on some of the most important issues facing people living today. It is a book about the nexus between ideas and their applications in ways that can improve our lives.

It begins by addressing the popular topic of happiness in Chapter 1 through an exploration of how the legendary proto-Daoist master Yang Zhu theorized happiness. It focuses on the Yang Zhu chapter of the Daoist classic *Liezi* which offers us a sophisticated treatment of the concept of happiness addressing a large number of inescapably foundational questions that can serve as metrics for evaluating theories of happiness in general. These questions include the *scope* of happiness, its *causation*, and its *purpose* as well as possible tensions between subjective and objective experiences, uniform and diverse causality, individual and collective outcomes, relative versus absolute happiness, and immediate versus lasting fulfillment.

Chapter 2 looks at the topic of health and longevity by examining the geographic hotspots or "blue zone" communities that have been discovered in Costa Rica, Greece, Italy, Japan, and the US. These are communities where researchers have found unusually high proportions of nonagenarians and centenarians. The chapter examines lifestyle observations and longevity prescriptions derived from studies of blue zone centenarians as compared to longstanding recommendations for the practice of nourishing life (*yangsheng*) to achieve a long and healthy life in the Daoist tradition. Comparative analysis reveals a very high degree of similarity across the four lifestyle domains of diet, exercise, mindset, and relationships. This correspondence seemingly validates many longstanding Daoist prescriptions for advancing health and longevity.

Chapter 3 is about consciousness and enlightenment. It puts forth a Daoist perspective on how humans can advance to a higher level of consciousness and ultimately become enlightened as articulated in the early Daoist classics of *Laozi* and *Zhuangzi*. It then turns to the writings of the influential "new age" spiritual teacher Eckhart Tolle whose books have sold millions of copies and have been translated into many languages. Both Tolle and the Daoists call for replacing the incessant stream of thoughts and judgments that we usually experience with a pure and empty mind that is fully in the present. The comparative analysis in this chapter exposes a strong resemblance between Tolle's writings and Daoist perceptions of consciousness and awakening. This overlap arguably reflects the latter's cross-cultural relevance and resonance over time.

Chapter 4 turns to ethics and specifically the ethics of a Daoist sage as gleaned from the *Wenzi*. The Daoist classics teach that individuals (and societies) have lost their way and become corrupted by falling into a tragic state of disconnectedness from the Way (*Dao*), the source of all life and creativity. The solution they offer emphasizes a sage or sages who (in contrast to most people) are in tune with the Way. But what exactly is the ethical character of a Daoist sage? In the classic of *Wenzi*, the eight principles of humility, relative obscurity, tranquility, sincerity, meditation, impartiality, loving-kindness, and emptiness/simplicity are highlighted as key features of Daoist sagely ethics. The *Wenzi*'s consistent emphasis on these principles reveals that the Daoist sage is not someone who is a-ethical or unethical while also distinguishing the Daoist sage ideal from competing prototypes of self-cultivation and virtuosity.

Chapter 5 concludes the book by offering a Daoist perspective on economics drawing upon the classical wisdom of Laozi's *Daodejing*. While scholars have offered differing interpretations over what a Daoist economic system ought to prioritize, this chapter focuses on three principles in accord with the Daoist concept of *yangsheng* (nurturing life). The first principle is embracing a circular economy in harmony with natural, environmental, and biological processes. The second is synergistically satisfying human needs. The third is meaningful work featuring worker autonomy, work-life balance, and optimal experience. Prioritizing mindfulness, time-freedom, and reproduction over capitalist production and accumulation, a Daoist perspective on economics provides us with key principles for reforming government policies and our lifestyles to engage in activities in harmony with nature rather than adopting some kind of *laissez-faire* or micro-interventionist economy.

In summary, this book illustrates multiple ways in which Daoist thought has been and can be practically applied to transform our individual modern lives and the structure of our societies. I hope you will enjoy it!

1 An Integrated Theory of Happiness

The Yang Zhu Chapter of the *Liezi*[*]

This opening chapter explores the integrated theorization of happiness associated with the legendary Chinese proto-Daoist figure of Yang Zhu as captured in the "Yang Zhu" 楊朱 chapter of the book named after the Daoist master Liezi 列子.[1] Rejecting the pursuit of political power, material gain, social status, and public reputation in favor of cultivating individual well-being, Yang Zhu was denounced as an amoral, pleasure-seeking hedonist by Confucian critics like Mencius.

In contrast, I argue that Yang Zhu's individually rational but socially non-conformist approach to well-being is of considerable relevance to contemporary scholarship on happiness. Not only does the Yang Zhu chapter of the *Liezi* offer us an intriguing and counter-intuitive argument about what constitutes and causes well-being, but its philosophy also addresses a large number of inescapably foundational conceptual questions that can serve as metrics for evaluating theories of happiness in general.

In recent decades, scholars have analyzed Yang Zhu's thought to better situate it vis-à-vis competing philosophical schools in China's Warring States period (475–221 BCE).[2] They have also examined changing perceptions of Yang Zhu from the Warring States period to the present.[3] As Carine DeFoort notes, the six prominent roles attributed to Yang Zhu in Chinese dynastic history range from "Yang Zhu as a rival in argumentation (late Zhou), a heretic (Han), a prominent figure in the *Liezi* (Wei Jin), a master with deficient thoughts (Song), and a political reformer (late Qing)" (2020: 237).

These roles have been followed more recently by the portrayal of Yang Zhu as a "philosopher" since the 20th century.[4] There is still, however, much dispute about what exactly Yang Zhu stood for (Brindley 2022). For instance, some label Yang Zhu as a hedonist (Graham 1989) or an egoist (Kushner

[*] This chapter was originally published in volume 17 of the *Journal of Daoist Studies* (see Joshi 2024a). The author would like to thank the editors of the journal for permission to reprint it here.

1980; Van Norden 2011), whereas others find Yang Zhu to be neither an egoist (Seo 2015) nor a hedonist (Li 2019; Liu and Li 2019).[5]

As argued here, irrespective of its particular position in moral, philosophical, and political debates of its era, the Yang Zhu chapter of Liezi is relevant to contemporary audiences because of its nuanced thinking about happiness and well-being. I explore that chapter's approach to theorizing happiness here in an effort to contribute to the growing international scholarship on interconnections between Daoism and happiness.[6]

To be clear, I am not offering a full-fledged Daoist theory of happiness nor endorsing all of Yang Zhu's prescriptions. Rather, my aim is to explain how a classical figure and text often associated with Daoism gives a message with rich implications for how we think about happiness. Instead of oversimplifying Yang Zhu into a predefined category such as egoist, hedonist, individualist, or Daoist, I explain how key ideas expressed in the Yang Zhu chapter of Liezi can inspire an integrated approach toward thinking about happiness.[7]

The rest of this chapter is structured as follows. It begins with a brief discussion of the legend of Yang Zhu and his core philosophy of "cherishing oneself." It then discusses how the narrative structure of the Yang Zhu chapter of the *Liezi* implies an integrated approach to theorizing happiness by addressing key issues regarding (a) scope (who, what, when, where), (b) causation (how), and (c) purpose of happiness (why). The Yang Zhu chapter also addresses a number of possible tensions in how we conceptualize happiness such as between subjective and objective experiences, uniform and diverse causality, individual and collective outcomes, relative versus absolute happiness, and immediate versus lasting fulfillment. As discussed in the chapter's conclusion, many of these foundational issues can serve as useful metrics for evaluating other theories of happiness.

The Legend of Yang Zhu

The legendary figure of Yang Zhu, also known as Yangzi 楊子[8] (c. 440–360 BCE), is often seen as a proto-Daoist figure representing the Yangist school of thought, which likely inspired a number of later Daoist thinkers (Graham 1989: 54). Similar to the modern psychological concept of "flow" (Csikzentmihalyi 1990), Daoists focus on optimal experience as an unselfconscious "state where the self is lost in the activity of following the Way" which means to be "in harmony with the Dao," the ultimate source of vitality that sustains life in the universe (Ivanhoe 2011: 139, 137; see also Zhang 2019).

Studying the Daoist sage Zhuangzi (c. 399–295 BCE), scholars find that "those who are in harmony with the Dao experience a sense of metaphysical comfort …. They feel a profound and special sense of security, peace, and ease as part of and party to powers much greater and grander than anything one could muster on one's own" (Ivanhoe 2013: 265). However, achieving this state of great "contentment" (Daniels 2019: 585) involving a "special feeling of satisfaction, ease, and delight" is typically out of reach or at least difficult for most of us to experience because our socialization "cuts us off and alienates us from the great Dao" (Ivanhoe 2013: 263, 276).

Textual Sources

Nobody really knows what Yang Zhu thought or did and such a person may have never even existed. A common claim is that Yang Zhu was a student of the Daoist sage Laozi (Wei 2019), but this shadowy figure's true origin remains unknown. Since Yang Zhu's original writings have been lost, what we know of his thought comes from exchanges preserved by others in texts such as the *Lüshi chunqiu* 呂氏春秋 (Mr. Lü's Spring and Autumn Almanac), an ancient encyclopedia stating that Yang Zhu "valued self" (Graham 2001; Chen 2012). As Villaver points out, the concept of self (*ji* 己) meant the opposite of others (*ren* 人) (2015: 218). Thus, some interpret Yang Zhu's thought as endorsing ethical egoism (Kushner 1980).

Yang Zhu is also mentioned in chapter 13 of the *Huainanzi* 淮南子 (Book of the Prince of Huainan), a syncretic text where he is associated with the doctrines of "keeping one's nature intact" (*quanxing* 全性), "protecting one's genuineness" (*baozhen* 保真), and "not allowing oneself to become tied to material things" (*bu yiwu leixing* 不以物纍形) (Fung 1983: 134; Graham 1989: 56; Fox 2008: 364). These three doctrines suggest that "being true to one's own natural destiny (*xing* 性) and avoiding attachments and hypocrisies that drain the body of its spiritual and physical resources will lead to the fulfilment of one's endowment" (Fox 2008: 364).

The *Huainanzi* also notes how Mencius opposed these doctrines and criticized the "excessive egoism" of Yang Zhu for supposedly championing the idea of acting only "for myself" (*weiwo* 爲我) (2008: 368). In a famous polemic, the Confucian scholar Mencius attacked Yang Zhu for being unwilling to "pluck one single body hair" (*yimao buba* 一毛不拔) to benefit "the world" (*tianxia* 天下) (Li 2010: 167).[9]

However, many contemporary scholars argue that Yang Zhu actually meant that one should not sacrifice one hair in exchange for receiving the benefit(s) of getting to rule the world (Graham 1989, 1990; Hansen 1992; Zhao 2014). In other words, one should not injure one's body (by removing even a single body hair) in the selfish pursuit of excessive wealth and power because "physical health is more important than anything – even the power of ruling a country" (Zhao 2022: 136). As Zhang (2020: 145) suggests, there is a kind of "'universalistic egoism' implied in Yang Zhu's philosophy. For Yang

Zhu, it is not only no harm to *my* hair to attain the world but also no harm to *anyone's* for the sake of attaining the world." By acting this way, "people do not infringe on one another, each content without being concerned with others' affairs, and the world naturally achieves order" (Li 2019: 124).

Yangist philosophy also appears in later parts of the *Zhuangzi* (a.k.a. Chuang-tzu), a Daoist collection formally edited around 300 CE by Guo Xiang (Graham 2001: 29). As Graham (1989: 55) notes, four of its chapters (28-31) on "Yielding the Throne," "Robber Chih," "Discourse on Swords," and "The Old Fisherman" probably belong to the Yangist school since they consist of "highly literary" dialogues with "much citation of instances from history and legend" producing stories "longer and technically more sophisticated than anything elsewhere in *Chuang-tzu*" (Graham 2001: 222). A prominent message in these chapters is that "the life of the body is more important than the things which serve to nurture it. Possessions are replaceable, the body is not," and one should be "careful not to be deluded into seeking power and possessions at risk to life by the two great temptations, greed for wealth and moral demand to contribute to the good government of the people" (ibid.).

Another significant textual source of Yangist philosophy and the one I focus on here is the chapter titled Yang Zhu in the *Liezi*, a text attributed to the legendary Daoist figure Lie Yukou 列御寇 (5th c. BCE), though the received version of this text dates to about 300 CE (Graham 1989: 60; Chen 2012: 1).[10] As scholars have noted, the *Liezi* anthology "is a compendium of hyperbolic anecdotes, seemingly paradoxical aphorisms, and curious parables" (Ames 2011: 1). The *Liezi*, which appears in the Daoist Canon, is often seen as the third most important Daoist work after Laozi and Zhuangzi (Graham 1990; Chen 2012). While the Yang Zhu chapter has sometimes been seen as anomalous within the *Liezi* (Graham 1990), scholars like Liu and Li (2019: 76) find "the 'Yang Zhu' chapter of the received *Liezi* is not only reliable, but also an especially valuable text – one that can serve as a foundational resource for study of Yang Zhu's thought." Hence, given the importance of the *Liezi* in Daoism and its inclusion of a separate chapter explicitly named after Yang Zhu, I focus on that chapter here. The chapter is also insightful because it implies a complex and integrated approach to thinking about happiness.[11]

Cherishing Oneself

A number of scholars have argued that Yang Zhu's most important contributions to thinking about happiness can be summed up as "cherishing oneself" (*guiji* 貴己) and "tending/nourishing life" (*yang sheng* 养生) (Zhao 2014: 173). As Fox notes, by prioritizing the "efficient preservation of life force," Yang Zhu's individual rationality was unconventional in its era by challenging social conformity and the hierarchically oriented, war mongering status quo (2008: 358). Graham describes Yangism as follows:

> [It was] a philosophy entitling members of the ruling class to resist the overwhelming moral pressures to take office …. But Yangism differs from its successors in having nothing mystical about it. It starts from the same calculations of benefit and harm as does Mohism, but its question is not "How shall we benefit the world?" but "What is truly beneficial to man?" more specifically "What is truly beneficial to myself?" Is it wealth and power, as the vulgar suppose? Or the life and health of the body and the satisfaction of the senses?
>
> (1989: 56)

By championing the idea of cherishing oneself, Yang Zhu shifted the empirical and normative unit of analysis regarding well-being and moral cultivation away from the family (as advocated by Confucians) and the state (as advocated by Mohists and Legalists) back to the individual.[12] As Zhao (2014: 174) notes, "Yang believed that if only everybody focused merely on taking care of themselves rather than others, the whole world could be in peace." In her view, Yang Zhu saw a need for us to abandon our "socialized external self" (*wo* 我) in favor of "returning to one's true internal self" (*ji* 己) (ibid.: 176). This implies keeping "one's physical body and sensual organs in a satisfied condition, one's mind and heart in a happy mood, and one's emotions and feelings in a pleasant situation" while cultivating "a natural attitude toward life and death; and a freedom from attachments to any conventional values or external material pursuits" (ibid.: 175).

An Integrated Theory of Happiness

The Yang Zhu chapter of *Liezi* holds much value for contemporary scholarship by signaling to us essential criteria for developing an *integrated* theory of happiness. This is because through its narrative format (of various stories and exaggerated characters), the chapter addresses many pivotal questions one might have regarding the meaning of "happiness" including its *scope* (i.e. who?, what?, when?, where?, how much?), *causation* (i.e. how?, why?), and *purpose* (i.e. why should it matter?). Dealing with these issues, the Yang Zhu chapter serves as a model for others by providing a series of metrics to use in developing an integrated theory of happiness (see Table 1.1). I will now examine these possibilities by discussing elements that an integrated theory of happiness ought to entail alongside examples of how the Yang Zhu chapter addresses those points.

What Is Happiness?

The first component an integrated theory of happiness ought to include is a clear explanation of the *meaning* it assigns the term "happiness" and its

Table 1.1 Metrics for Evaluating an Integrated Theory of Happiness

#	Issues to Settle	Possible Tensions Within Each Issue
1	What is Happiness? (meaning, intension)	Subjective vs. Objective
		Emic vs. Etic
		Authentic vs. Artificial
		Image vs. Substance
		Happy vs. Not Unhappy
		Presence vs. Absence
		Positive vs. Negative (framing)
		Reality (*sein*) vs. Appearance (*schein*)
		Hedonic (pleasure) vs. Eudaimonic (flourishing)
		Affect vs. Cognition
2	Happiness of whom? (unit of analysis)	Self vs. Others
		Individual vs. Collective
		Humans vs. Sentient Beings
		Living vs. Dead Persons
3	Happy when? (temporality, duration)	Past vs. Present vs. Future
		Process vs. Product
		Momentary vs. Intermittent vs. Sustained vs. Whole Life
		Short-term vs. Long-term
		Quality vs. Quantity of Life
		Upward vs. Downward Trajectory
4	Happy where? (spatiality)	Internal (mind) vs. External (body)
		Differentiated vs. Integrated Domains
		Multiple vs. Single
		Holism vs. Part-ism
5	Happy by how much? (degree, depth)	Shallow vs. Deep
		Active vs. Passive
		Dichotomous vs. Continuous
		Summative vs. Average
6	Happy why and how? (causation)	Mental (consciousness) vs. Material (resources)
		Mind vs. Body
		Uniformity vs. Diversity
		Mono-causal vs. Multi-causal
		Homogeneity vs. Heterogeneity (equifinality)
		Necessary, Sufficient, or Conducive Conditions
		Set-points/Inheritance vs. Actions/Agency
7	Why be happy? (purpose)	Intrinsic (ends) vs. Instrumental (means)
		Normative vs. Empirical/Positive
		Critical vs. Distant/Disengaged
		Being Good vs. Feeling Good

intension. For example, its conceptualization of happiness should distinguish between its major (essential/core) and minor (peripheral/optional) components. In the Yang Zhu chapter, the essential components of happiness are made clear – to be physically (body) and mentally (mind) healthy and satisfied, free from worries or stress, and in touch with and able to live in accordance with one's own unique nature. This philosophy is embodied in the phrases "cherishing/valuing self" and "tending/nourishing life" which refer to "the satisfaction of personal needs without injuring health and life" (Graham 1990: 143). Thus, in response to a rich and a poor person both of whom had bad experiences, Yang Zhu responds that "the right course ... is to be found in enjoying life, in freeing ourselves from care. Hence those who are good at enjoying life are not poor, and those who are good at freeing themselves from care/worry do not get rich" (1990, 141).

In this respect, Yang Zhu's conceptualization of happiness implies hedonic balance. On the one hand, he advocates "simply living without restraint; do not suppress, do not restrict" enjoyment of the pleasures of the senses including music and song (hearing), beautiful women (seeing), flowers and spices (smelling), discussing truth and falsehood (expressing and contemplating), fine clothes (touching), and good food (tasting) (1990: 142). On the other hand, one should exercise a degree of moderation in such enjoyment in order to live a tranquil life and to be able to continue enjoying such pleasures while living out the full life course nature has prepared for us (Chen 2012: 52).[13]

By contrast, the opposite of this ideal consists of being trapped in stressful situations, being coerced to do something that goes against one's health and internal nature, and pursuing external "pseudo-satisfiers" (Max-Neef 1992: 205–209) like wealth and reputation which appear on the surface to make us happy but might actually fail to do so. Thus, Yang Zhu's conception of happiness includes both objective criteria (health) and subjective elements (feeling free of stress) as well as affective (feeling pleasure) and cognitive (feeling content) dimensions. It combines short-term enjoyment of various pleasures and long-term enjoyment of how nature has made us.

In response, one might ask how can one know whether a person is truly happy or not? This raises two important considerations. The first concerns a potential gap between *sein* (reality) and *schein* (appearance). This relates to the difference between genuine happiness as opposed to that which looks like happiness but is actually just a social expectation or something illusory. For instance, society may laud and praise those who are good looking, are star athletes, or have big salaries when those attributes may be simultaneously unrelated to or even detrimental to a person's happiness if they take time and energy away from things which would generate greater happiness.[14]

A second important concern is issue framing. Are we talking about "being happy?" or "not being unhappy?" This subtle distinction is important because researchers have found framing things positively (focusing on the presence of something good) versus negatively (emphasizing the absence of something bad) significantly impacts how people perceive and evaluate outcomes (Kahneman 2012). Yang Zhu's integrated approach circumvents this potentially confounding aspect by incorporating both positive and negative framing to discuss causes of happiness (following one's inherent nature, etc.) as well as causes of unhappiness. Regarding the latter, he states: "People find no rest because of four aims – long life, reputation, office, possessions. Whoever has these four aims dreads spirits, dreads other men, dreads authority, dreads punishment. I call him 'a man in flight from things'" (Graham 1990: 154).

Whose Happiness?

Secondly, an integrated theory of happiness ought to address the question of whose happiness we are talking about. An important distinction here is whether the *unit of analysis* is an individual (me or her) or a collective (us or them). There is a possible tension here because my (or her) happiness may come at the expense of your (or their) happiness. Likewise, your (or their) happiness may come at the expense of my (or her) happiness.[15]

Following the principles of cherishing oneself and "cherishing the body" (*guishen* 贵身), Yang Zhu responds to this issue by placing emphasis on the individual's happiness. The reason for this choice is because the happiness of the individual may ultimately be the cornerstone for the happiness of everyone. As Zhao explains,

> If each person's own distinctive nature can be recognized and respected, external and international conflicts will be dramatically reduced and the violence and terrorism that result from hate and revenge will be eradicated. If everybody/every country can focus on their internal business and internal cultivation based on their own nature, and not focus on disturbing, intervention, and the control of other countries, then the world could really be in peace.
>
> (2014: 185–186)

As this attempt to aggregate Yang Zhu's principle of cherishing oneself reveals, the Yang Zhu chapter of *Liezi* rejects hypocritical, repressive, and unproductive moralities imposed on societies and individuals. According to Yang Zhu, "there is an old saying that each of us should pity the living and abandon the dead. This saying puts it exactly. The way to pity others is not simply to feel for them. When they are toiling we can give them ease, hungry we can feed them, cold we can warm them, in trouble we can help them to get through" (Graham 1990: 141–142). As this passage illustrates, Yang Zhu was in favor of supporting all life (both ours and his), leading A.C. Graham to conclude that Yang Zhu "wants pleasure for other men as well as for himself" (1990: 136).[16]

As Zhao (2014: 180) likewise notes, in Yang Zhu's vision "pursuing one's personal enjoyment should not be based on the rejection of taking care of others … *Yang sheng* (养生, nourishing life) should include both the nourishing of one's own life and that of others" (ibid.: 180). Thus, Graham (1989: 54, 55) defends Yang Zhu as someone "concerned for life in general, not just his own" and as "an individualist concerned to benefit his own person and

Table 1.2 Self and Others in Theories of Happiness

	Self wins	*Self loses*
Other wins	1) Win (self) + Win (other)	3) Lose (self) + Win (other)
Other loses	2) Win (self) + Lose (other)	4) Lose (self) + Lose (other)

leave others to do the same." This stems from Yang Zhu's belief that altruism is unrealistic. Whereas gods or heroic mythical figures like the legendary Chinese emperors Shun and the Great Yu may have been capable of altruism, such behavior would be impossible for mere mortals. Hence, Yang Zhu seeks to advance both individual and collective well-being, but if the two come into conflict, he prioritizes the well-being of one's self. Thus, Yang Zhu's preference hierarchy as shown in Table 1.2 is option 1 > option 2 > option 3 > option 4. The preferred (best) solution is win-win over win-lose. The second-best would be win-lose and so on.

Happiness When?

A third issue to address in an integrated theory of happiness concerns *when* a person is happy (or when should they be happy) and for *how long*? There is a potential tension between being happy in the present (now) or the past (then) versus being happy in the future (later). One should perhaps also consider whether our happiness is on an upward or downward trajectory over time and whether happiness should be viewed as a process or a product. There is also a possible tension in the *duration* of happiness – whether it is limited to a given moment (instantaneous, fleeting), whether it comes and goes (intermittently) or whether it is lasting (continuous, sustained). For instance, one may experience happiness in the short term but not in the long term. It is also possible that experiencing happiness in the future might require us to undergo sacrifices (i.e. unhappiness) in the meantime.

Yang Zhu's integrated approach fortunately provides answers to a number of these questions concerning temporality. Firstly, the Yang Zhu chapter appears to favor hedonic balance so that an individual can enjoy happiness both now and in the future. If there is a conflict between the present and the future, however, it advocates pursuing happiness now instead of waiting for later.

> While you are alive, resign yourself and let life run its course, satisfy all your desires and wait for death. When it is time to die, resign yourself and let death run its course; go right to your destination, which is extinction. Be resigned to everything, let everything run its course; why need you delay it or speed it on its way?
>
> (Graham 1990: 148)

In Yang Zhu's perspective, life is so short that one should live for enjoyment (now) instead of working to build a social reputation (Graham 1990: 135–137). Yang Zhu starts from the premise that most people unfortunately spend their entire lives in a miserable state, and the immanence, inevitability, and universality of death is emphasized repeatedly in the following passages.

> A hundred years is the term of the longest life, but not one man in a thousand lives so long. Should there be one who lives out his span, infancy and senility take nearly half of it. The nights lost in sleep, the days wasted even when we are awake, take nearly half the rest. Pain and sickness, sorrow and toil, ruin and loss, anxiety and fear, take nearly half of the rest. Of the dozen or so years which remain, if we reckon how long we are at ease and content, without the least care, it does not amount to the space of an hour.
>
> (Graham 1990: 139)

> We all die; saints and sages die, the wicked and foolish die.
>
> (1990: 140)

> Make haste to enjoy your life while you have it; why care what happens when you are dead?
>
> (1990: 141)

As these passages illustrate, although Yang Zhu valued both quality of life and quantity of life, to him the former is more important. One of his disciples expounded on this by stating that having no life is better than a miserable life; "to keep one's life intact is the best, to keep one's life partially completed is the second, death is the next, and to live under force is the worst one" (Zhao 2014: 179). Yang Zhu's emphasis on quality of life is illustrated in his story of Tuanmu Shu of Wei who upon receiving a generous inheritance "followed his impulse and did as he pleased ... Whatever his passions inclined him to enjoy, whatever his ear wished to hear, his eye to see and his mouth to taste, he would send for without fail" (Graham 1990: 146). But Tuanmu Shu also shared what he had with many others. When he got older, he "gave away all the precious things in his treasuries and storehouses, all his carriages and robes and concubines" and possessed nothing when he died (1990: 147).

Happiness Where?

A fourth issue worth addressing in an integrated theory of happiness concerns *where* in our lives do we experience happiness? Is it localized in certain specific domains (happy with my job, happy with my finances, happy with my love life) or globalized across all domains (happy with everything)? Relatedly, is happiness something experienced by our mind or body or both? Here again, there is potential for conflict as someone might experience pleasure in their body but torture in their mind or conversely contentment in one's mind but pain in one's body.

On this issue, Yang Zhu sees happiness as a matter of both mind and body. He wants pain to accrue to neither the body (not losing a single hair) nor the mind (does not want an ounce of stress). One might also ask whether happiness is an instantaneous response (affective) or an overall evaluation (cognitive), and Yang Zhu sees it as a matter of both. While pleasure-seeking, Yang Zhu does not appear to endorse hedonic (pleasure) happiness over *eudaimonic* (flourishing) well-being.[17] Rather, his ideal is for individuals to enjoy both forms of well-being. As Zhao (2014: 184) observes, Yang Zhu subscribes to "a life cherishing philosophy based on the satisfaction of both one's physical and psychological, as well as spiritual needs."

How Happy?

A fifth issue relevant to an integrated theory of happiness is how much or to what extent one ought to be happy. Relatedly, how does one know whether someone has achieved that degree of happiness? These issues concern epistemology (how we know something exists) and measurement (determining how much of something is present). Regarding the latter, there are possible tensions between taking subjective (self-appraisal) as opposed to objective (externally observable indices) approaches to measuring happiness. This overlaps to some extent with differences between emic (insider perspective) and etic (outside perspective) approaches to understanding phenomena.

One might also like to have a sense of whether one's measures are valid, reliable, and replicable. When we talk of a person's happiness, are we talking about an absolute level of happiness or a happiness level relative to some other person's happiness or external benchmark? Correspondingly, what is the distribution of happiness across a society or societies?[18] Then there is the important issue of "how much is enough?" and "How much does it take to be happy?"[19]

While the Yang Zhu chapter does not provide answers to all of these questions, on the crucial issue of how much one needs to be happy, Yang Zhu evidently champions the idea of diminishing marginal returns – that you only need enough of certain things to be happy and that getting more than enough will not make you any happier. On this he remarks,

> A grand house, fine clothes, good food, and beautiful women – if you have these four, what more do you need from outside yourself? One who has them yet seeks more from outside himself has an insatiable nature. An insatiable nature is a grub eating away one's vital forces.
>
> (Graham 1990: 156)

Why Are Some People Happy?

An integrated theory of happiness should address what makes people happy. What generates happiness? And more broadly what *causes* things to happen in this world? Are outcomes determined primarily by mental (consciousness) or material (resources) sources/factors?

Yang Zhu's answer is that fulfilling both mental and material needs matters for our happiness. Yang Zhu believes in getting pleasure out of material things but is also against being tied to material things and rejects blindly following social conventions (Fox 2008: 367).[20] A related issue is to what degree happiness is influenced by inherited/genetic "set points" (nature) or by our interactions with the world and people around us (nurture). In this respect, Yang Zhu sees it as a matter of both. He contends that "struggling against one's natural inclinations takes a great deal of work, and this stress dissipates our energies and vital resources" (ibid.: 367). At the same time, Yang Zhu believes we can say no to what society wants from us and turn away from the lure of status, possessions, and fame. He stresses the role of agency and the importance of individuals choosing to step off the hedonic treadmill.

Yang Zhu teaches us that the route to happiness is multi-causal, much like various "list theories" of happiness (Haybron 2013: 85) and in contradistinction to mono-causal theories which assert there is only one primary cause of happiness. Yang Zhu also seemingly supports the idea of equifinality – that there may be multiple routes to happiness given that each individual is different. Given Yang Zhu's conception that "each individual's destiny is unique" (Fox 2008: 363), his theory is more aligned with causal heterogeneity/diversity as opposed to causal homogeneity/uniformity.

The complexity of Yang Zhu's causal thinking is reflected in his view that happiness involves both subjective and objective as well as individual and collective dimensions. The intersection of these dimensions produces four quadrants (see Table 1.3) related to the individual's interior (intentional) and exterior (behavioral), and the collective's interior (cultural) and exterior (social) states of being (Wilber 2000: 70). Thus, when it comes to individual subjective happiness, consciousness may be a primary determinant of happiness. For instance, are we content with and appreciative of what we have? For our collective subjective happiness, however, ideology and shared beliefs may play a larger role. As for individual objective happiness, resources

Table 1.3 Four Dimensions/Levels of Causal Forces in Happiness Theories

	Individual Happiness	Collective Happiness
Subjective Happiness	I. Individual Consciousness	II. Shared Beliefs
Objective Happiness	III. Personal Resources	IV. Social and Natural Environment

(i.e. financial, material, emotional, technological, etc.) that are at one's own disposal may be primary determinants. Lastly, in terms of our collective objective happiness, the surrounding environment (social, political, natural, and economic) in which we find ourselves may play a significant role.

Why Try to Be Happy?

A final issue worth including in an integrated theory of happiness is the *significance* and *relevance* of happiness vis-à-vis other possible aims or goals in life. Happiness may be a worthwhile pursuit, but for some people, certain things such as kindness, goodness, health, meaningfulness, longevity, wealth, morality, power, responsibility, children, or success may be valued more than happiness.[21] Moreover, the value of happiness may differ across individuals and societies. Some may see it as a supreme value, whereas others may not value it at all. For some, happiness is of *intrinsic* value (as an end in itself), whereas for others, it holds *instrumental* value (as a means to achieving something else).

In this respect, not only does the Yang Zhu chapter of *Liezi* make empirical claims about what causes happiness (staying out of public affairs, following one's inherent nature, etc.), but it also normatively champions happiness as a (more) desirable aim vis-à-vis other potential life goals such as pursuing a social reputation, power, or wealth (Graham 1990). A representative passage in a Yangist chapter of Zhuangzi captures this prioritization.

> The petty man will die for riches, the gentleman will die for reputation … in so far as they throw away what is already theirs and are willing to die for something that is not theirs, they are identical … Do not be a petty man – return to and obey the Heaven within you; do not be a gentleman – follow the reason of Heaven … Turn your face to the four directions, ebb and flow with the seasons.
>
> (trans. Watson 1968: 334)

As the quote illustrates, in Yang Zhu's vision, one should use things in this world "to nourish one's nature" when in fact regrettably "most are using their natures to nourish other things" (Graham 1989: 57). For Yang Zhu, the happiness gained by cherishing oneself and following one's inherent nature is of intrinsic value and hence superior to things like acquiring wealth, rank, and reputation which have only instrumental value. As Zhao (2014: 181; see also Slingerland 2000) contends, "Yang Zhu has actually suggested a new moral standard here. To follow one's internal nature is not evil but a true virtue; the spontaneous internal nature should be where the true morality comes from."

As the Yang Zhu chapter of Liezi states, "Man resembles the other species between heaven and earth, and like them owes his nature to the Five Elements … However, my body is not my possession; yet once born, I have no choice but to keep it intact" (Graham 1990: 153). As the Yangist viewpoint emphasizes, human lives and human bodies are not our own. They are essentially on loan from Heaven and therefore we must be responsible for fulfilling our duty to nourish our bodies, meet its needs, and keep it alive for the duration Heaven has planned for us. We are not to treat our bodies or lives as possessions as if they were "ours" or to subject ourselves to harm or excesses that will damage what Heaven has given us.

Conclusion

While Yang Zhu was criticized by ancient critics for supporting the happiness of individuals over the interests of the state or family, "Yang Zhu's rejection of public life and dedication to self-cultivation, originally a bold minority position, became widely persuasive" (Emerson 1996: 546). A possible shortcoming of Yang Zhu's approach is that its individualistic orientation might run into a fallacy of composition, but it is clear that the Yang Zhu chapter of Liezi also favors collective well-being and only rejects those social practices which come at the expense of fulfilling the individual's vital needs. Moreover, Yang Zhu's integrated approach rejects extremism. For instance, he sees the mind-body distinction as counterproductive as both the mind and the body matter for human well-being.[22] On this and many other matters, the Yang Zhu chapter brings different elements of life together in a coherent fashion. Hence, it provides us with the building blocks to develop an *integrated* theory of happiness that incorporates hedonic balance to avoid artificially reducing or extending our life span.

Drawing from Yang Zhu's thought enables us to develop a checklist of items for evaluating theories of happiness in general. Yang Zhu's theorization of happiness has many pioneering insights such as how framing effects perceptions of happiness as prospect theory has recently rediscovered. For instance, the framing of "benefit the world" as opposed to "gain the world" elicits vastly different responses. Yang Zhu was also attentive to time horizons, discount rates, and depth perception regarding how soon death will come and take over us. While seemingly individualistic on the surface, a deeper analysis as shown here reveals Yang Zhu's simultaneously collective orientation. For instance, all of the putatively hedonist characters in Yangist writings were opposed to violence – revealing his humanist, non-violent, and life-nurturing approach. The fact that these and so many other complexities are woven into his theorizing makes Yang Zhu's approach both subtle and nuanced.

Were future studies to work toward developing more explicit, comprehensive, and integrated theories of happiness, the Yang Zhu chapter of Liezi is arguably a good model to follow as few since have come up with such a sophisticated theory. For instance, its thinking, which takes both *whose* happiness and *when* into consideration, gives us several possible combinations where a happiness theory might fall. Optimal happiness would presumably

Table 1.4 Spatiality (Scope) and Temporality (Time) of Happiness

	Unit: Individual	Unit: Collective
Time: Present	1 (Me, now)	2 (Us, now)
Time: Future	3 (Me, later)	4 (Us, later)
Time: Present + Future	5 (Me, now + later)	6 (Us, now + later)

be option #6 (as shown in Table 1.4) which can be described as a "win-win-win-win" because it entails happiness for us (both you and me) always (both now and later).[23] This denotes happiness over a greater time span and for more people compared to other options in Table 1.4 which are more restrictive by being limited only to a single individual or point in time. On this matter, it seems Yang Zhu's first choice would be option #6 and that he would retreat to option #1 only when a more comprehensive (i.e. shared and sustained) happiness were not feasible. By contrast, it seems many contemporary approaches to happiness as advocated by "positive psychology" are limited only to focusing on option #1 while giving much less consideration to other possibilities.

To conclude, Yang Zhu's integrated theory of happiness is one that normatively promotes individual well-being as an ultimate goal in life.[24] This made his controversial approach stand out compared to his contemporaries because happiness differs in kind from other attributes such as kindness, goodness, meaningfulness, longevity (i.e. quantity of life),[25] wealth, morality, power, responsibility, and success.[26] The challenge for Yang Zhu is not how to balance happiness against such other possibly desirable goals, but how to achieve happiness and sustain it. His answer seems to emphasize that we follow (a) our own internal nature, (b) adopt hedonic balance to enjoy well-being both in the moment and in the future, and (c) when possible also support the well-being of others. From the Yangist view, if we rationally think it through we will reject much of what society wants us to do – i.e. pursuing longevity, rank, reputation, office, power, and wealth.[27] Instead if we just listen to our inner nature and live naturally as Heaven made us, we will flow unhesitatingly and smoothly through life like water flowing in a river.

Notes

1 According to Fox, the label "proto-Daoist" refers to "ideas that exert some influence on the emergence of a distinguishable Daoist tradition" (2008: 358).
2 For example, Kushner (1980), Graham (1989, 2001), Hansen (1992), Emerson (1996), Fox (2008), Zhao (2014), Villaver (2015), Zhang (2020), Defoort and Lee (2022), and Brindley (2022).
3 See Cao (2019), Chen (2019), He (2019), Li (2019), Liu and Li (2019), and Wei (2019).
4 Recent evaluations of Yang Zhu's philosophy include an edited volume by Defoort and Lee (2022) and a 2019 special issue in the journal *Contemporary Chinese Thought*.

5 Still others find Yangism itself containing two opposing camps – one of "indulging" and the other of "restraining" one's "inborn disposition and nature" (Cao 2019: 147).

6 See Chiang (2009), Chen (2010), Davis (2011), Ivanhoe (2013), Joshanloo (2014), Tiwald (2016), Lobel (2017), Daniels (2019), Zhang (2019), and Zhao (2022). On the relationship between Daoism and psychology more generally, see Cohen (2009) and Kohn (2011).

7 As Cao contends, Yang Zhu has been slotted into various imposed categories but "such doctrinal thinking seems to first choose a shirt and then squeeze the body into it" (2019: 159).

8 In classical texts, Yang Zhu's name appeared in several forms such as: 楊朱, 楊氏, 楊子, 陽子, 陽生, 陽居. See Chen (2019: 92) and Wei (2019: 141).

9 As Li notes, the high status conferred upon Mencius in the Song Dynasty added to Yang Zhu's negative reputation, a classic irony given that Yang Zhu never cared about reputation anyway (2019: 120).

10 The chapter title is translated as "Yang Chu" by Graham (1990).

11 Translations from the Yang Zhu chapter of *Liezi* that follow are from Graham (1990).

12 While Schwartz's interpretation is that Yang Zhu represents historical fatalism (1985: 188), Graham views Yang Zhu as an advocate for people "to live out the term of life which Heaven has destined for man" (1989: 56).

13 For Yang Zhu, "to injure health by excess or risk life to multiply possessions is to forget that things are only means to the life generated in us by Heaven; one's possessions are replaceable, one's life is not" (Graham 1989: 57).

14 Yang Zhu cautioned against "identifying with the unreal (fame, luxury, tradition) at the expense of the real (nature, the body)" (Emerson 1996: 546).

15 Such tensions are not only found in happiness theories but also in many variants of liberalism which do not always support everyone's freedom and even condone harming some to benefit others (Joshi 2020).

16 In Emerson's view, "Yang Zhu did not liberate the 'individual' from his obligations. What he did was to elevate private affairs (both family and personal) above public business" (1996: 550).

17 The concepts of *eudaimonia* and *hedonia* originated in ancient Greece. According to Huta, the former includes "states and/or pursuits associated with using and developing the best in oneself, in accordance with one's true self and one's deeper principles. Hedonia includes states and/or pursuits associated with pleasure and enjoyment, and the absence of pain and discomfort" (2013: 201).

18 As well-being researchers have observed, this kind of measurement – especially when trying to compare happiness levels across cultures can be very difficult (Tov and Au 2013).

19 I would like to thank Matthew Hammerton for raising these great points.

20 As Alan Fox notes, "meditation, conscious breathing exercises, and vigorous physical activity" will help the individual "to develop a clearer sense of what exactly *is* the 'good life,' and to have the courage and integrity to follow that course through to the end, despite the alienation and social censure that may ensue" (2008: 369).

21 For instance, some people believe it is more important to "be good" than to "feel good."

22 As expressed by Yang Zhu, a body needs its pleasure which comes from material things just as a mind needs its contentment which comes from its state of consciousness.

23 The sixth option here would be even more impactful if "us" refers not to a small subset ("my family," "my business," "my university," or "my nation") of a broader population but to everyone (i.e. "the world" or "humanity" or "all sentient beings").

24 In an integrated theory of happiness, the meaning of happiness as de-contested by the theory should also be distinguishable from other potentially desirable outcomes. For instance, "happiness" is sometimes used interchangeably by researchers with "quality of life," "subjective well-being," and "life satisfaction," but scholars have warned against conflating happiness with concepts such as "goodness," "development," or "progress" (Stewart 2014).

25 Interestingly, the Yang Zhu chapter of Liezi downplays longevity as a goal in life in contrast to the many "yangsheng" focused Daoist religious texts providing guidance on achieving longevity (Joshi 2021).

26 Illustrating this difference, Haybron (2013: 101) notes how icons like Martin Luther King and Mother Teresa may be "exemplars of meaningful lives," yet were not necessarily happy. Yang Zhu likewise discusses how ancient Chinese sage kings like Shun and Yu are universally admired, but their actual life experiences must have been miserable (Graham 1990: 150).

27 In this respect, Yangism differs slightly from the Daoism of Zhuangzi as the latter places emphasis on abandoning conscious thought (in favor of mystical insight) to achieve optimal experience.

2 The Way of Longevity

Blue Zones as Models of Daoist Living[*]

In recent years, researchers have endeavored to identify geographic regions around the world with unusually high proportions of nonagenarians and centenarians in order to distill general lessons for how people everywhere can live long and active lives with minimal impediments. Thus far, studies of these longevity hotspots or "blue zones" have concluded that certain community norms and practices may contribute up to a decade of prolonged healthy living (e.g. Buettner 2012; Poulain, Herm and Pes 2013; Buettner and Skemp 2016). Not surprisingly, these claims have attracted much attention among scholars and the general public (e.g. Appel 2008; Buettner 2012; Poulain et al. 2013; Carter 2015; Buettner and Skemp 2016; Hitchcott, Fastame and Penna 2018).

To Daoists, however, such ideas are far from novel. With over 2,000 years of wisdom gained in the search for immortality, Daoism has functioned almost like an applied science of longevity in China (and beyond) having acquired much knowledge from mystical insights, sacred scriptures, shared reflections, and experimental processes of trial and error (e.g. Wong 1997; Engelhardt 2000; Ai 2006; Kohn 2009, 2012; Zhao 2016; Davis 2018). As the Daoist tradition has already invested much time and effort into identifying social and lifestyle determinants of longevity, this chapter compares Daoist recommendations for the practice of "nourishing life" (*yangsheng* 养生) with longevity prescriptions derived from studies of blue zone centenarians.[1] If the two are similar, it would suggest that Daoists may have been right all along.

Blue Zones as Longevity Hotspots

In demographic research, the term "blue zone" denotes "a rather limited and homogeneous geographical area where the population shares the same

[*] This chapter was originally published in volume 14 of the *Journal of Daoist Studies* (see Joshi 2021). The author would like to thank the editors of that journal for permission to reprint it here.

DOI: 10.4324/9781003517344-2

lifestyle and environment and its longevity has been proved to be exceptionally high" as measured by ratios of healthy nonagenarians and centenarians to the overall population (Poulain et al. 2013: 89). Thus far, the following five blue zones have been identified across four continents based on the work of Dan Buettner (2012; also Buettner and Skemp 2016).

Ogliastra, Sardinia (Italy). The first blue zone is in a remote, mountainous part of the island of Sardinia in the Mediterranean Sea where people often have to work long hours and walk long distances to "eke out a living from a rugged land by raising sheep and goats" (Buettner 2012: 39). Having long experienced economic isolation, this region retains many "traditional social values, such as the respect for elders as a source of experience, the importance of the family clan, and the presence of unwritten laws" (2012: 35). Unlike the rest of Italy, this region has experienced exceptional longevity with one out of every 200 people born between 1880 and 1900 becoming centenarians (Franceschi and Bonafè 2003: 457). Men and women centenarians are also equal in number unlike most industrialized countries where women significantly outnumber men when it comes to reaching old age.

Nicoya Peninsula, Costa Rica. This historically isolated region in the northwest of Costa Rica features a group of villages exhibiting exceptional longevity. Though not materially wealthy, residents are family-oriented, work on the land, soak up much sun, and eat nothing packaged or processed. As one local centenarian acknowledged, "he loved to work, mostly because the fruits of his labor have provided for his family. For most of his career, he worked as a mule driver, hauling logs out of the forested hills and acting as a courier across the largely road-less Nicoya Peninsula. He also grew corn, beans, and vegetables to feed his wife and six children" (Buettner 2012: 188). Consuming a mostly vegetarian diet, the elderly inhabitants here, many of whom descend from Chorotega Indians, are characterized by a strong work ethic, "zeal for family" (2012: 180) and have "apparently lived low-stress lives" (2012: 192).

Okinawa, Japan. The islands of Okinawa, a formerly independent kingdom now part of Japan, have unusually high life expectancy, especially for women. Okinawa experienced heavy destruction during World War II and scarce food resources before the war, yet despite these hardships, as Dan Buettner argues, older Okinawans were almost "born into a lifestyle that promotes health. They have been blessed by access to year-round fresh, organic vegetables, strong social support, and these amazing herbs that amount to preventive medicines" (2012: 95). Busy working, gardening, engaging in social activities, and maintaining their households into their late years, Okinawans belong to close knit social groups called *moai* (模合) with whom they meet regularly throughout their lives for mutual support.

Ikaria, Greece. Like Okinawa, Ikaria is a fairly remote island that suffered greatly during World War II. Its landscape is rocky and mountainous, but perhaps due to remarkably fresh air, water, and a low stress lifestyle, this longevity hotspot features "as many healthy males over 90 as females that age" (Buettner 2012: 240). Located in the Aegean Sea, the food here is fresh and local – a variation of the Mediterranean diet – and people frequently visit their neighbors to share conversations and wine. Featuring "exceedingly low rates of dementia" (ibid.: 244), residents share a sense that life is more important than money and that people should support each other.

Loma Linda, California. This community of Seventh Day Adventists living in Southern California features life expectancy ten years higher than the US national average. As in other blue zones, religious beliefs play an important role in people's lives. Early morning prayers, regular exercise, and a day off each week from work and technology – the Sabbath – for long hikes with family and friends reinforce people's social connections and relationship with nature. Adventists consume a mostly Biblical diet prioritizing nuts, legumes, fruits, vegetables, and salads while generally avoiding processed foods, meat, alcohol, smoking, and caffeinated beverages.

Aside from these five longevity hotspots, there are now efforts to bring blue zone lifestyles to other parts of the world including cities and towns in the US and Canada. The first US Blue Zones' "demonstration community" was in Albert Lea, Minnesota, in 2009. The so-called Blue Zones Project in its promotion of longevity efforts has worked together with various municipalities in the country, seeking "to transform ordinary American towns into extraordinary places where people live long, healthy lives: the Blue Zones" (Carter 2015: 376).[2] Some optimists even believe that with appropriate lifestyle modifications, especially in diet and nutrition, "blue zones, now limited to just a few populations in the world, can become commonplace" (Appel 2008: 215).

Daoist Longevity

There may be a correspondence between blue zone lifestyles and the Daoist longevity tradition, which strongly emphasizes cultivation of physical health to achieve a long and healthy life. As Yanxia Zhao states,

> At the heart of Daoism is the strong focus on happy and healthy longevity ... the aim of Daoist religion is to encourage its practitioners to attain the Dao, and to achieve Oneness with this great Source of all living things, and thus become an immortal or a true being. In this way, Daoism affirms the capability of humans to become a transcendent being by their own personal effort.
>
> (2015: 131)

Livia Kohn notes that while the Chinese traditionally believed that human life has a "predetermined duration of 120 years ... Daoists have always claimed that there are not only ways to reach this life expectancy on a regular basis but to extend it to far longer periods" (2009: 85). Stressing human agency, a popular Daoist saying is that "my life is in my hands, not in the hands of Heaven" (Wang and Yan 2017: 154).[3] They hold that to a large extent, whether one lives "with a strong physical body or a weak one, with a short lifespan or a long one, is entirely dependent on oneself" (Zhao 2015: 132).

As championed by classical Daoist texts including Zhuangzi 庄子, Liezi 列子, and *Taiping jing* 太平经 (Scripture of Great Peace), Daoists have long prioritized the ideal of nourishing and nurturing life as well as related aims of "nourishing inner nature" (*yangxing* 养行) to achieve "longevity" (*shou* 寿), and "long life" (*changsheng* 长生) (Kohn 2012: 3).[4] Many Daoists also believe the human body is "a microcosm with the physical features of the world or universe as macrocosm" serving as "a sort of 'vessel' or 'residence' of the Dao" (Engelhardt 2000: 95–96). To them, the body serves as a reservoir of "a vital energy known as *qi* (气), which can be described as a bioenergetic potency that causes things to live, grow, develop, and decline" (Kohn 2012: 4). Human life is the accumulation of *qi*, while death is its dispersal. As Kohn explains,

People constantly draw *qi* into the body from air and food as well as from other people through sexual, emotional, and social interaction. But they also lose *qi* through breathing bad air, living in polluted conditions, overburdening or diminishing their bodies with food and drink, getting involved in negative emotions, engaging in excessive sexual or social interactions, and in general suffering from various forms of stress.

(2012: 4)

Managing one's *qi*, therefore, is considered essential to longevity, and traditional "practice focuses relentlessly on the internal *qi* of the body; longevity is the reward for maintaining *qi* harmoniously in its circulation" (Michael 2015: 158).[5]

In the Daoist tradition, practices of nourishing life advance across three levels from healing illnesses through extending longevity to achieving immortality (Engelhardt 2000: 80; Kohn 2012: 9; Zhao 2015: 132; Zhao 2016: 202). The most advanced stage is immortality which is an objective of Daoist "internal alchemy" (*neidan* 内丹) and involves intensely ascetic practices. By contrast, beginner and intermediate level "self-healing and self-health-care exercises" for those whose aim is to extend life by a decade or two can be "practiced by ordinary people in their daily lives and activities" (Zhao 2015: 132). Thus, Daoist cultivation is more akin to the Chinese concept of "preserving health" (*baojian* 保健) by preventing diseases from occurring in the first place than the more modern and Western-influenced idea of "medical treatment" (*yiliao* 医疗), that is applied only after one has already been afflicted.

Daoist conceptualizations of nourishing life have transformed over time. The earliest methods, recorded in the Han dynasty and before, worked primarily with breathing, bodily exercises, and alchemical experiments (see Michael 2015). Later they evolved to include techniques that involve both body and mind (see Wong 1997; Engelhardt 2000; Zhao 2014, 2015, 2016).[6] In addition, the ideal of nourishing life with its longstanding Daoist connotations increasingly became common in popular discourse, so that today it is frequently used in the promotion of goods and services designed to alleviate various forms of "diminished health" (*yajiankang* 亚健康) (Bloch 2019: 171).[7] More specifically, longevity practices relevant to daily living and improved health can be applied in four lifestyle domains: diet, exercise, mindset, and relationships.

Diet and Exercise

While Daoist lore is full of "recipes for ingesting herbs and minerals for immortality" (Wong 1997: 38), entry-level Daoist dietetics heavily emphasize eating food that is natural, not preserved, freshly cooked, and in season (Kohn 2012: 177; see also Arthur 2009; Kohn 2010, 2013).[8] Consuming healthy foods grown locally is encouraged, and diets should be primarily plant-based with minimal fat and meat (Wong 1997: 228).[9] Although total conversion to vegetarianism is not required, one should eat lightly and in small portions remembering to "always leave a bit of room in the stomach, eating lightly especially at night, and to balance the intake of food with movement – ideally a walk of a mile or so after a meal – so that digestion can work properly" (Kohn 2012: 177).

As for other ingestible substances, Daoists do not prohibit medicinal supplements or liquor, but these should be consumed in moderation as food, herbs, and minerals are preferable to drugs for strengthening and healing the body (Engelhardt 2000: 93).[10] In this way, eating healthy foods is seen as a means of "food as medical treatment" (*shiliao* 食疗) to prevent the onset of a disease and ill health (Dear 2012: 20). Daoists also like to "absorb fresh *qi*" (*fuqi* 服气) from sources such as clean air, dew, and mist, and to absorb the "essence of the sun and moon" (Wong 1997: 44). Those seeking to reach more advanced stages of immortality cultivation will eventually seek to

> wean themselves from solid food, replacing it with raw vegetables, fruits, and nuts ... They then increase herbal supplements, liquid nourishment, and internal guiding of *qi* ... to the point where they no longer need food but live entirely on *qi*. This process, called "abstention from grain" [*bigu* 辟谷], lightens the body's structure in favor of subtler energies and cosmic awareness.[11]

> (Kohn 2009: 87)

Such austere measures, however, are not expected of ordinary people who eat grain-based meals and are more focused on yin-yang balance (Kohn 2010: 74).[12] In addition to longer life, expected benefits of Daoist dietetics include "clear eyesight, acute hearing, strong bones and muscles, supple flesh, black hair, being light, being invigorated, and having all of one's teeth ... [basically] overcoming the manifestations of an aging body" (Arthur 2009: 45).

Aside from dietary measures, Daoist longevity techniques include calisthenics to enhance flexibility, increase strength, make the body lighter, and promote smooth *qi*-flow.[13] An important feature of classical practice is "*qi*-circulation, specified as 'spitting out the old and taking the new [*qi*]' (*tugu naxin* 吐古纳新) plus healing exercises or *daoyin* 导引 (lit. guide and pull) bends and stretches modeled on animals, such as the typical 'bear-hangings and bird-stretches' (*xiongjing niaoshen* 熊泾鸟申)" (Michael 2015: 146).[14] The latter also include the "five animals frolic" (*wuqin xi* 五禽戲) and other animal-based postures.[15] Many of these "*qi* exercises and postures," nowadays summarily called qigong 气功, can be "incorporated into the daily activities of sitting, standing, walking and laying down. Thus, cultivating the body can occur in every facet of life" (Wong 1997: 218; see also Engelhardt 2000: 83).[16]

Another energy practice used for long life is taiji quan 太极拳 (a.k.a. t'ai chi), an internal martial art utilizing "low-impact, slow-motion exercise" accessible to all including "the sickest and most elderly, even those confined to wheelchairs or recovering from surgery" (Zhao 2016: 205).[17] Other forms include the "eight brocades" (*baduanjin* 八段锦) and "diamond longevity practice" (*jingang changshougong* 金刚长寿功) which help *qi* flow through the body's meridians (Zhao 2016: 205). Beyond this, there are various forms of massage, kneading, and specific forms of sexual practice, known as the "bedchamber arts" (*fangzhongshu* 房中术).

Daoists encourage the practice of both "external strengthening" (*waizhuang* 外壮) and "internal strengthening" (*neizhuang* 内壮) exercises. The former maintains healthy muscles, ligaments, tendons, and blood circulation using techniques such as tendon-stretching and marrow-washing, while internal strengthening works on the "internal structure and functions of the physical body ... massaging the internal organs, enhancing the circulation of blood, and stimulating the nervous system" (Wong 1997: 178).[18] For the most part, "Daoist exercises consist of slow movements and careful stretches combined with deep breathing and conscious awareness. Releasing stress, alleviating heaviness, aiding digestion, and improving circulation, they open the energy channels, balance yin and yang, and activate a subtler dimension of being" (Kohn 2009: 88).

Mind and Society

Traditionally Daoists view the body and "heart and mind" (*xin* 心) as fully integrated and inseparable. To enhance health, they accordingly highly emphasize meditation and breath regulation and control.[19] For example,

Wong (1997) discusses a dozen different types of Daoist meditations including various forms of visualization, concentration, and observations (see also Kohn 2009: 88). The aim of these different methods is to reach "a state where the mind has been freed from desires and is completely absorbed in Dao" (Kohn 2012: 264). Related techniques include "standing and moving *qigong* (subtle breath skills), *neigong* (inner mind skills)" as well as the "inner smile and sitting in oblivion," all of which aim to reduce or eliminate chronic stress and increase "overall well-being" (Zhao 2016: 205).

To maintain a healthy mindset, Daoists have long "advocated living a simple lifestyle with minimal desire, believing that too much excitement and satisfaction of the senses could harm body and mind" (Wong 1997: 28; see also Kohn 2009: 87; Kohn 2012: 78; Bloch 2019: 165). Insisting on "the importance of stilling the mind and dissolving desire," Daoists generally believe "the ultimate reality of Dao can be experienced only by the original mind, which is empty of thoughts, attachments, and desire" (Wong 1997: 71, 83). Hence, early Daoist philosophers like Zhuangzi who famously "regarded social conventions as the greatest enemy of personal freedom and integrity" avoided occupations mired by greed and hypocrisy (ibid.: 26). The basic point is "people should avoid stress" (Kohn 2009: 87).

Although Daoism is an "individual focused tradition" (Zhao 2015: 125) that historically opposed those socially imposed rules which are incompatible with a being's inherent nature (Kohn 2009: 92), it also stresses "harmonious relationships among individuals" and "between individual and society" (Zhao 2015: 125). As Eva Wong notes, resembling the shamans of ancient times, the original notion of a "Daoist sage was also a very involved member of the community … far from doing nothing, the Daoist sage of the *Daode jing* 道德经 is an active member of society and is fit to be a king" (1997: 24–25).

The role of community also varies across different branches of Daoism with some placing considerable emphasis on "accumulating merit by doing charitable works" as it is believed that "good deeds bring reward and unethical deeds invite retribution" (Wong 1997: 6). An important text from the Song dynasty laying out moral admonitions is the *Ganying pian* 感应篇 (Treatise on Impulse and Response). It states

> If you are in harmony with the Dao you will advance … Be kind and compassionate to all things. Be dedicated in whatever you do … Help orphans and widows. Respect the old and care for your young. Do not hurt trees, grass, and insects. Share in the suffering of others. Delight in the joys of others. Help people in desperate need. Save people from harm. View the good fortune of others as your good fortune. View the losses of others as your own loss.

(Wong 1997, ch. 4: 191)

Supporting people in need, volunteering without taking credit, and being loving to all creatures under heaven are also implied by Daoism's "three treasures" of "kindness" (*ci* 慈), "simplicity" (*jian* 俭), and "not daring to be ahead of the world" (*bugan wei tianxia xian* 不敢为天下先) (Zhao 2015: 128). Daoism encourages each individual person to "establish a harmonious relationship with her/his natural and social environment, and also with the other species on earth and in the universe" (Zhao 2015: 126; see also Miller 2017). Lastly, on a more intimate level, Daoists encourage people to have healthy sexual relations to enhance their well-being and produce healthy children (e.g. Ai 2006; Dear 2012). Especially important is hedonic balance and *qi* maintenance, that is, to enjoy sexual excitement but to not over exhaust one's energy supply (Kohn 2009).[20]

Comparison

Comparing Daoist longevity prescriptions with those derived from studies of blue zone centenarians, Dan Buettner's "power nine" recommendations are most relevant. He developed them based on his interviews in the five longevity hotspots and describes them as "a cross-cultural distillation of the best practices of health, a de facto formula for longevity" (2012: 5). Related to Daoist practices, they are displayed in Table 2.1.

Diet. The "power nine" list includes three dietary recommendations: cut calorie intake by 20%, eat plant-based foods while avoiding meat and processed foods, and drink red wine (in moderation – e.g. one to two glasses per day). These recommendations largely parallel those of Daoism. The first, caloric restriction, is a type of fasting that cuts down the amount of calories consumed compared to a normal diet and helps to maintain a healthy body weight (Buettner 2012: 259). For instance, Okinawans try at every meal to stop eating when their stomach is 80% full by uttering the phrase "*hara*

Table 2.1 Longevity Recommendations from the Blue Zones

Dimension	Blue Zones – "The Power Nine" Recommendations
A. Diet	1) "*Hara Hachi Bu*" – cut calories by 20%.
	2) "Plant Slant" – avoid meat and processed foods.
	3) "Grapes of Life" – drink red wine (in moderation).
B. Exercise	4) "Move Naturally" – balance, walking, regular low-intensity physical activity, be active.
C. Mindset	5) "Purpose Now" – take time to see the big picture.
	6) "Downshift" – take time to relieve stress.
	7) "Belong" – participate in a spiritual community.
D. Relationships	8) "Loved Ones First" – make family a priority.
	9) "Right Tribe" – be surrounded by those who share blue zone values.

Source: Author's adaptation from Buettner (2012).

hachi bu" 腹八分, before each meal to remind themselves of this objective.[21] Similarly, Ikarians practice occasional fasting, while Nicoyans and Loma Lindans eat light dinners. Daoist *yangsheng* dietetics likewise involve calorie restriction by emphasizing light eating and engaging in the practice of leaving the stomach up to one third empty when eating meals (Kohn 2010: 76).

The blue zone recommendation to eat a diet strong in fresh vegetables, fruits, legumes, and nuts so as to provide the body with sufficient vitamins and nutrients also resembles early-stage Daoist dietary practices which favor vegetarian, fresh, non-processed, and locally grown foods. In both traditions, meat is eaten infrequently (ranging from once or twice a week to once a month or never) and, as in typical Chinese diets, the meat most commonly eaten in (four out of five) blue zones was pork.

In each specific blue zone, local foods, herbs, and minerals often obtained from home gardening, local foraging, beekeeping, fishing, and animal husbandry were associated with longevity (see Table 2.2). As with Daoism's focus on the importance of herbs and minerals for longevity, Ikarians enjoy wild medicinal teas; Okinawan centenarians ate a diet rich in herbs, calcium, vitamins, and iron; and Nicoyans drank hard water rich in calcium and magnesium. Further resembling Daoist attention to building strong bones through practices like marrow-washing, blue zone residents consume items rich in calcium, such as goat's milk and cheese in Sardinia and nuts in Loma Linda.

Table 2.2 Health Promoting Local Foods in the Blue Zones

Blue Zone	Health Promoting Local Foods by Region
1) Sardinia (Italy)	Goat's milk, whole wheat, red wine from Cannonau grapes, garden vegetables, mastic oil, and beans.
2) Okinawa (Japan)	Sweet potatoes, tofu and fermented soy products, green tea, bitter melon (*goya*), daikon radish, mugwort, turmeric, miso soup, herbs, and garden vegetables.
3) Loma Linda (USA)	Nuts, whole grains, tomatoes, legumes like peas and beans, and drinking lots of glasses of water every day.
4) Nicoya (Costa Rica)	Fresh tropical fruit from one's own yard (e.g. papaya, mango, chico zapote, oranges), corn infused with lime, beans, squash, garden vegetables, high-antioxidant vitamin-rich foods (e.g. manon, anona, wild ginger), and mineral rich (in calcium and magnesium) hard water.
5) Ikaria (Greece)	Dark honey, herbal teas, local yogurt, olive oil, potatoes, goat's milk, beans, wild greens (such as fennel, dandelion and horta), bread, locally caught fish consumed about twice a week, and drinking two to four gasses of red wine per day.

Source: Author's compilation from Buettner (2012).

Table 2.2 highlights specific local foods considered to be health promoting in the blue zones. Growing, raising, and collecting one's own food is emphasized in the *yangsheng* tradition and venerated in classical Daoist texts. In the same way that Ikarians eat wild greens growing around their island, Daoists have traditionally foraged for immortality elixirs from herbs, minerals, and metals in the wild.

Other blue zone recommendations include drinking wine and lots of water plus absorbing sunshine. While liquor was absent from Nicoyan and Adventist diets, wine from grapes or rice (Japanese *sake*) is regularly consumed in Sardinia, Ikaria, and Okinawa. Thus, imbibing alcohol does not seem to be necessary for longevity, but having the right kind of drink in the right context may beneficially release stress. This is compatible with the Daoist preference for moderation in ingesting strong substances like alcohol.[22] An equivalent to drinking lots of water is the Daoist tendency to consume lots of tea – a practice motivated by the fact that water generally needs to be boiled in order to be potable in China and adding tea leaves enhances the taste of boiled water (Kohn 2010: 90). Lastly, sun exposure which allows the body to soak up Vitamin D is found among centenarians in blue zones especially in sub-tropical Okinawa and tropical Nicoya. This is something traditional Daoists would have likewise enjoyed while spending time meditating on mountain tops and engaging in organic gardening (Blofeld 1978). Moreover, since the Daoist creed holds that absorbing the sun's energies is good for one's *qi*, some Daoist practitioners deliberately expose themselves to direct sunlight – though preferably at sunrise or sundown when the light is least blinding (Wong 1997).

Exercise. Another blue zone recommendation is to "move naturally" on a regular basis and maintain a healthy body mass index (BMI) by engaging in cardiovascular activities to absorb oxygen and raise the heart rate, antigravity practices like walking and standing, balancing through activities like yoga and taiji quan, and strength training to build and maintain muscle mass (Buettner 2012: 16–18). Likewise, strength, flexibility, and balance exercises are emphasized in Daoist methods of nourishing life, and certain qigong forms demanding slow movements and careful stretches resemble body movements that commonly occur in blue zone activities like gardening in Nicoya and Okinawa and shepherding in Sardinia.[23]

In the blue zones, elders typically "engage in regular low-intensity physical activity, often as part of a daily work routine" (2012: 267). Examples include the unselfconscious workout one naturally gets from working in the garden, tending sheep, repairing the house, or walking to the market. Other blue zone recommendations, like always taking the stairs, walking or bicycling instead of driving, or sweeping with a broom instead of using automated cleaning devices, also resemble Daoist preferences for more nature-conforming tools and methods over the use of technologies that are highly divorced from nature or which require extensive imported fuels and which generate waste, noise, and pollution.

Walking is also ubiquitous in the blue zones and appeared to be "the one activity that all successful centenarians did – and do – almost daily" (Buettner 2012: 269). Regularly walking long distances "has a positive effect on muscle and bones – without the joint-pounding damage caused by running marathons or triathlons" (2012: 60). In Daoism, walking is also a preferred means to get to places. Aside from the long walks and hikes Daoists have historically taken in remote mountains to find natural ingredients, Laozi reminds us that a "thousand-mile journey begins with a simple step" (ch. 64).

Mindset. Another more mind-focused takeaway from the blue zones is that one should live with a sense of purpose, take time to see the big picture, relieve stress, downshift, and participate in a spiritual community. These points are likewise emphasized in Daoism. As for having a purpose in life, Dan Buettner explains that "Okinawans call it *ikigai* [in Japanese: 生きがい], and Nicoyans call it *plan de vida*, but in both cultures the phrase essentially translates to 'why I wake up in the morning'" (2012: 281). Daoists are likewise well-attuned to the bigger picture concerning their own position within the cosmos. They have a crystal-clear purpose in life: to follow, return to, merge with, and become one with Dao.

Daoists also typically participate in a spiritual community whether they are monastics who "leave the family (*chujia* 出家), lay disciples following a particular religious master (*sujia dizi* 俗家弟子) or still in society (*shehuishang* 社会上)" (Bloch 2019: 178). Just as Daoists are devoted to their spiritual beliefs and practices, blue zones centenarians demonstrated great devotion and commitment in their faith and prayers. They were not only religious and accepting of life circumstances but exhibited considerable positivity and appreciation.[24] For instance, in Nicoya, the centenarian

> Panchita's faith was amazing – her unwavering belief that no matter how bad things got, God would take care of everything. Indeed, thinking back, I realized that most of the 200 centenarians I had met believed in a similar guiding power. The Seventh-day Adventist faith was rooted in a strong faith tradition; Okinawan elders believed that their deceased ancestors watched over them; and Sardinians were devout Catholics.
>
> (Buettner 2012: 209)

While subscribing to differing faith traditions, what blue zone centenarians have in common is that they "tend to relinquish control of their lives to God" and "go through life with the peaceful certitude that someone is looking out for them" (2012: 210). Daoists likewise believe in surrendering themselves to Dao as captured by the "spiritual ideal known as *wu wei* [無爲], that is, non-action or effortless action" (Ivanhoe 2011: 127). This implies that instead of relying on one's conscious mind, one allows a supernatural insight or intuition to help one along in life (see Graham 1989).

Practicing downshifting and minimizing stress, blue zone centenarians are "wise enough to know that many of life's most precious moments pass us by if we're lurching blindly toward some goal" (Buettner 2012: 284). For instance, in Ikaria, people make time for spontaneity and the community shares the belief that people should work to live rather than live to work. Following the principles of "contentment" (*zu* 足) and being "free from desire" (*wuyu* 無欲), Daoists likewise stress the value of life over money even if much of society leans the other way (Joshi 2020).[25]

As one Ikarian exclaimed, people here "wake up late and always take naps … Have you noticed that no one wears a watch here? … We simply don't care about the clock here" (Buettner 2012: 234–235). Likewise, prioritizing simplicity, reducing stress, and minimizing materialism, Daoists would rather spontaneously submit to nature's clock than to rigidly adhere to man-made divisions of time.

Relationships. Research on the blue zones suggests that social connectedness contributes positively to longevity with the "power nine" telling us to make family a priority.

The most successful centenarians we met in the Blue Zones put their families first. They tended to marry, have children, and build their lives around that core. Their lives were imbued with familial duty, ritual, and a certain emphasis on togetherness … Their lifelong devotion has produced returns: Their children reciprocate their love and care. Their children check up on their parents, and in four of the five Blue Zones, the younger generation welcomes the older generation into their homes.

(Buettner 2012: 290–291)

In the blue zones, elders are not abandoned but rather taken care of by younger family members, especially daughters and granddaughters, and there is respect for the aged. Thus, many elders feel "a strong sense of service to others" and they actively "care for their family" (2012: 190).

Although family does not receive much emphasis in classical Daoist texts, respect for elders resonates with Daoism (Ai 2006: 155). While there are legendary stories of Daoist hermits living extensively long lives, John Blofeld's experience living among Daoist monastics suggests that they still form a community even after they leave ordinary society and dedicate themselves to self-cultivation (1978). These communities are different: "Daoists aim to set themselves apart from ordinary society, creating communities that are clearly distinct" (Kohn 2010: 71).

On another level, Daoists value the healthy integration of sexuality in one's life. This echoes the blue zones feature of long-lasting marriages and life-partners who support each other.[26] The unmistakable presence of children and grandchildren among blue zone centenarians also connects with ideals of nourishing life, given that conceiving healthy children is "naturally one of the oldest and most basic objectives of *yangsheng*" (Dear 2012: 22).

Another blue zone recommendation is to surround yourself with others who share "blue zone values." "This is perhaps the most powerful thing you can do to change your lifestyle for the better" and "it's much easier to adopt good habits when everyone around you is already practicing them" (Buettner 2012: 293–294). The three island regions (Okinawa, Sardinia, and Ikaria) and remote peninsula (Nicoya) have limited contact with the outside world, making this easier to achieve, but even in Loma Linda in Southern California, "most Adventists seem to hang out with other Adventists" (2012: 161). In these communities, reinforcement of values within the group and geographic region appears to foster longevity-enhancing lifestyle behaviors and practices. As one Ikarian explains,

> In Samos [a neighboring island], they care about money. Here we don't. For the many religious and cultural holidays, people pool their money and buy food and wine. If there is money left over, they give it to the poor. It's not a "me" place. It's an "us" place.
>
> (2012: 235)

Like many blue zone centenarians, Daoists similarly take "a non- ego-centered approach to the world ... [although] formulating a personal rather than social ideal, they support compassion, love, generosity, and openness toward all" (Kohn 2009: 93).

Conclusion

Comparing Daoist prescriptions for longevity with those based on blue zones research, I found a very high degree of overlap across the four lifestyle domains of diet, exercise, mindset, and relationships.[27] In fact, many lifestyle recommendations associated with successful aging in the blue zones not only resemble but also validate multiple longstanding Daoist prescriptions for advancing health and longevity.

Following nature and encouraging nourishing life practices for oneself as well as for other people and all living beings is an important principle in Daoism.[28] Similarly, blue zone centenarians are found living close to nature, tending gardens, raising sheep, going for long hikes, eating plant-based diets, and living in non-technological spaces. For instance, in Sardinia, many centenarians "had worked hard their whole lives as farmers or shepherds. Their lives unfolded with daily and seasonal routines. They raised families who were now caring for them. Their lives were extraordinarily ordinary" (Buettner 2012: 40).[29]

Spending time in nature and away from urban mega-conglomerations is characteristic of both traditional Daoist practitioners and contemporary blue zone centenarians. Both prefer to spend ample time in the wilderness, mountains, and remote natural areas, that is, in places unperturbed by man-made pollution and noise. This allows them to breathe in the freshest air and absorb the healthiest *qi*.

Valuing and setting aside time to spend in nature is further reinforced by the community. Thus, Adventist communities reinforce their values by taking an entire day off every week from the modern world of work and technology to relax, pray, and go on nature walks with family and friends.[30] Aside from reducing physical and psychological stress, such partial delinking from domi-nant norms of modern societies may facilitate longer and healthier lives. Here again parallels with Daoism are obvious: Daoists are true champions when it comes to taking time away from the hectic pace of industrial and urban soci-ety for purposes of meditation, friendship, and nature immersion.

Another important takeaway from blue zone centenarians is the multiple benefits obtained from integrating healthy practices into everyday life. Gar-dening is a prime example. "Working in a garden requires frequent, low-inten-sity, full-range-of-motion activity. You dig to plant, bend to weed, and carry to harvest. Gardening can relieve stress. And you emerge from the season with fresh vegetables – a Blue Zones trifecta!" (Buettner 2012: 269).

Similarly, integration is a prominent theme in *yangsheng* exercises, many of which combine physical movements, breathing, and meditation or mental focus. This sort of integration likewise appears in Daoist ritual performance:

> Prostrations, bows, and walking patters are designed to open blockages in the spinal column and move energy from the base of the spine to the top of the head. In addition, the alternation of kneeling, standing, prostrating, and bowing is an excellent way to strengthen tendons and bones, maintain flexibility and mobility, and keep the energy flowing.
>
> (Wong 1997: 169)

On a final note, centenarians in the five blue zones do not seem to have received much influence from Daoist theology, nor is there much evidence of them having an explicitly Daoist awareness. Nevertheless, to a large extent, they appear to reflect spontaneous and natural models of Daoist living as they incorporate many activities and behaviors resembling nourishing life practices into their daily lives. It seems that in blue zones, without being conscious of it, many people have been simply and naturally following the Dao of longevity.

Notes

1 Livia Kohn (2012: 1–2) distinguishes between "longevity (healthy old age) and pro-longevity (radical life extension) that may lead eventually to immortality (freedom from death)." As she points out, efforts to achieve both "work in two main thrusts: personal lifestyle modifications and advanced medical research. The former … works mainly with diet (especially calorie restriction), supplements (vitamins,

growth hormones), exercise (aerobics, weight training, stretches), and stress reduction (relaxation, meditation)."

2 The Blue Zones Project has worked with at least 27 cities across the US (Buettner and Skemp 2016: 321). See: https://communities.bluezonesproject.com/

3 This Daoist saying hails from the Baopuzi 抱朴子 compiled by Ge Hong 葛洪.

4 Other formative Daoist texts emphasizing *yangsheng* include the *Yangsheng fang* 养生方 (Recipes for Nourishing Life), *Yangsheng lun* 养生论 (On Nourishing Life), *Yangsheng yaoji* 养生要集 (Compendium of Nourishing Life Essentials), *Baopuzi yangsheng lun* 抱朴子养生论 (Baopuzi on Nourishing Life), and *Yangxing yanming lu* 养性延命录 (Record on Nourishing Inner Nature and Extending Life). See Engelhardt (2000), Kohn (2012), and Zhao (2016).

5 Harmony, both within the body and in society, has long been championed by various movements in China including the Chinese government's campaign over the past decade to build a "socialist harmonious society" (Joshi 2012).

6 By the Song dynasty (960–1279 CE), Daoists had abandoned their earlier experiments with "external alchemy" (*waidan* 外丹) in favor of more internal "dual cultivation of body and mind" (Wong 1997: 79).

7 As Dear (2012: 12) notes, in China today "the two-character phrase [*yangsheng* 养生] embellishes the advertising and merchandising of everything from jars of honey to saunas and spas, country villa sales or indeed tourism promotion for cities and whole provinces."

8 Foods believed to have special healing properties that were traditionally chopped and mixed into immortality pills include asparagus root, atractylis, China root fungus, Chinese lyceum (gouji), jade bamboo, malva, pine tree, sesame, and Solomon's Seal (Kohn 2012: 121).

9 The main reason for meat avoidance is negative impacts on the body's health (Kohn 2010: 83).

10 To avoid strong tastes and flavors, *yangsheng* dishes often are "lightly cooked and mild in flavor ... the principle is to avoid overstimulation" (Dear 2012: 19).

11 Daoist monastics consume a more restrictive diet (Kohn 2010: 77–79).

12 Yin foods tend to grow in dark spaces, whereas yang foods grow in the light (Kohn 2012: 117).

13 The *Daoyin jing* (导引经) is an early source of many such healing exercises (Kohn 2012: 98).

14 Animal postures are good to emulate because "animals are beings of the natural world that have not sacrificed their inner natures to the dictates of socialization. Their systems of bodily circulation are open, whereas efforts toward the external world to gain power, wealth, or fame draw a human's attention away from the body and create blockages in the rhythmic, internal systems of circulation, leading to early death" (Michael 2015: 146).

15 The "five animals" are tiger, deer, bear, monkey, and crane. By contrast, "the *Daoyin jing* presents various practices associated with ... mostly water-based creatures, such as toad, turtle, and dragon" (Kohn 2012: 97).

16 Popular with many older Chinese people, "the energy exercise qigong, which is heavily influenced by Daoism" can benefit one's "blood sugar levels, insulin levels, microcirculation, and disease resistance" (Ai 2006: 157–158).

17 Other internal martial arts to "stretch the tendons, articulate the joints, soften the muscles, and improve general circulation" include "eight trigrams palm" (*baguazhang* 八卦掌), "form and intention fist" (*xingyiquan* 形意拳), and the "six harmonies and eight methods" (*liuhe bafa* 六合八法) (Wong 1997: 225).

18 "Needless to say, these movements require precise execution, or injuries can occur" (Wong 1997: 213).

19 Regulating breath is without conscious control, whereas "directing breath" is conscious control over breathing. Methods of regulating the breath include nostril

breathing, mouth and nostril breathing, mouth breathing, natural abdominal breathing, reverse abdominal breathing, perineal breathing, tortoise breathing, fetal breathing, and breathing with the entire body (Wong 1997: 214–216).

20 As Wong explains, "generative energy [*jing* 精] is produced in sexual arousal … Thus, to conserve generative energy, one must be sexually aroused but not emit the procreative substance" (1997: 185). In order to achieve this, one must "engage in sexual techniques whose aim is to revert the flow of the *jing* from down and out to up and in, thus using it to 'nourish the brain' (*huanjing bunao* 还精捕脑)" (Engelhardt 2000: 99).

21 Consciousness also contributes to dietetics in both Okinawan and Daoist contexts. As Arthur's study of classical Daoist practices reveals, a meal's health effects are strongest when adepts are "aware of the medicinal and *qi*-based properties of the ingredients they are ingesting … this requires adepts to be cognizant of their own energetic needs when choosing an appropriate diet" (2009: 35).

22 While advanced Daoist practitioners often forgo alcohol consumption, "'nourishing life liquors (*yangshengjiu* 养生酒) are long established in longevity and Daoist practice" (Bloch 2019: 176).

23 Okinawan centenarians exhibiting good body strength and balance appear to have regularly gardened, collected firewood, sat on the floor, and engaged in kneeling and squatting – for instance, using squat toilets. Similarly, lifestyle practices involving physical activity such as home and landscape maintenance, cooking, or working as a nurse and giving massages were credited with contributing to longevity in Loma Linda (Buettner 2012: 147–151).

24 In some blue zones, the predominant religious doctrine also prioritizes healthy longevity as with Adventists who believe "God wants us to be healthy" (Buettner 2012: 138), thereby providing a strong (i.e. divinely inspired) motivation to engage in healthful living.

25 In line with Daoist expectations, no centenarians mentioned in Buettner's blue zone interviews appeared to be lawyers, politicians, economists, business executives, or hailing from other high-stress, high-paying occupations with the exception of one nonagenarian medical surgeon.

26 As for sexual intimacy, Buettner suggests in passing how some blue zone elders may still be having active sex lives. For instance, in Ikaria people live long and "die quickly, often in their sleep, and – occasionally – after sex" (2012: 251).

27 The point here is not to minimize differences across places, peoples, and traditions but to highlight what appears to be great commonalities when it comes to advancing longevity.

28 Daoists emphasize "nature" (*ziran* 自然) both in terms of one's internal disposition and the natural environment (see Liu 2011; Wang 2015; Miller 2017).

29 The obscurity of these centenarians resembles how Daoist sages seek to avoid fame (e.g. Graham 1989).

30 As one Loma Lindan interviewee mentioned, "It reminds us that we don't need to have all the answers, that we recognize our finite capabilities, and that we are dependent on God" (Buettner 2012: 150).

3 Consciousness and Enlightenment

A Daoist Reading
of New Spiritual Teachings

How can a person transform their consciousness to experience enlightenment? Over the past few decades, new religious movements and spiritual leaders have attracted international attention for their answers to this perennial question. But what is the relationship between these contemporary teachings and Daoism (a.k.a. Taoism)? In the case of East Asia, we now find several new religions such as Cao Dai in Vietnam, Weixin Shengjiao in Taiwan, and Daesoon Jinrihoe in Korea which explicitly incorporate Daoism or specific Daoist elements into their theology and practices.[1] But what about new religious and spiritual movements outside East Asia? Has Daoism influenced them as well?

As there is considerable diversity among new religions, it is not possible to provide a complete answer to that question here. But this chapter sheds some light on this issue by comparing Daoist views on consciousness and enlightenment with that of a very influential Western contemporary New Age spiritual teacher named Eckhart Tolle (1948–). Tolle's teachings are known for drawing from various religious traditions of the world without aligning closely with any single denomination, but I contend that Tolle's view of enlightenment actually closely mirrors a long-standing Daoist perspective. I demonstrate this by comparing Tolle's pronouncements on spiritual enlightenment in his best-selling books, *The Power of Now* (1997/2004) and *A New Earth* (2005), with Toshihiko Izutsu's (1984) theorization of the "perfected man" in the Daoist classics of Laozi (老子) (a.k.a. Lao-tzu) and Zhuangzi (庄子) (a.k.a. Chuang-tzu).

Eckhart Tolle is a prime example of an influential New Age spiritual teacher. In his books, which have sold millions of copies and have been translated into many languages, Tolle claims that human beings have two purposes in this world. Firstly, all people share the same inner and primary purpose which is to gain a higher state of consciousness. He insists that working to attain this is by far the most important thing in our life. Secondly, each individual has a different outer purpose but one that "is always

DOI: 10.4324/9781003517344-3

relative, unstable, and impermanent" and this is much less important than our inner purpose (Tolle 2005: 264). As Tolle describes it,

> The true or primary purpose of your life cannot be found on the outer level. It does not concern what you do but what you are – that is to say, your state of consciousness. So the most important thing to realize is this: Your life has an inner purpose and an outer purpose. Inner purpose concerns Being and is primary. Outer purpose concerns doing and is secondary ... Your inner purpose is to awaken. It is as simple as that. You share that purpose with every other person on the planet – because it is the purpose of humanity. Your inner purpose is an essential part of the purpose of the whole, the universe and its emerging intelligence. Your outer purpose can change over time. It varies greatly from person to person. Finding and living in alignment with the inner purpose is the foundation for fulfilling your outer purpose. It is the basis for true success. Without that alignment, you can still achieve certain things through effort, struggle, determination, and sheer hard work or cunning. But there is no joy in such endeavor, and it invariably ends in some form of suffering.
>
> (Tolle 2005: 258)

As highlighted in the passage above, the most important thing for people at all times is to focus on their consciousness. As Tolle notes, "Whenever you become anxious or stressed, outer purpose has taken over, and you lost sight of your inner purpose. You have forgotten that your state of consciousness is primary, all else secondary" (ibid.: 266).

Tolle argues that in order to bring our consciousness to a state of enlightenment, we must let go of thinking about time and become exclusively focused on the present, in what he calls "the Now." This means completely stopping our dwelling on either the past or the future which is what we usually do and what he sees as the great affliction of humanity. As Tolle asserts, "the more you are able to honor and accept the Now, the more you are free of pain, of suffering – and free of the egoic mind" (2004: 33). Achieving this awakening and freedom requires extinguishing the ego which generally controls our minds. As Tolle argues,

> All negativity is caused by an accumulation of psychological time and denial of the present. Unease, anxiety, tension, stress, worry – all forms of fear – are caused by too much future, and not enough presence. Guilt, regret, resentment, grievances, sadness, bitterness, and all forms of non-forgiveness are caused by too much past, and not enough presence.
>
> (Tolle 2004: 61)

> The elimination of time from your consciousness is the elimination of ego ... We are, of course, not referring to clock time ... [what] we are

speaking of is the elimination of psychological time, which is the egoic mind's endless preoccupation with past and future ... The ego cannot tolerate becoming friendly with the present moment, except briefly just after it got what it wanted. But nothing can satisfy the ego for long. As long as it runs your life, there are two ways of being unhappy. Not getting what you want is one. Getting what you want is the other.

(Tolle 2005: 207)

To eliminate ego, Tolle argues that we must begin to listen to the voice in our head and recognize that it is not us. We can then let go of thoughts just as easily as they enter our head. As he states, "*be* there as the witnessing presence. When you listen to that voice, listen to it impartially. That is to say, do not judge. Do not judge or condemn what you hear, for doing so would mean that the same voice has come in again through the back door" (Tolle 2004: 18). As he explains,

Thinking and consciousness are not synonymous. Thinking is only a small aspect of consciousness ... but consciousness does not need thought. Enlightenment means rising above thought, not falling back to a level below thought, the level of an animal or a plant. In the enlightened state, you still use your thinking mind when needed, but in a much more focused and effective way than before. You use it mostly for practical purposes, but you are free of the involuntary internal dialogue, and there is inner stillness.

(Tolle 2004: 23)

The evidence Tolle provides in support of these claims draws primarily upon his own lived experience through which he personally came to experience an enlightened consciousness. As he states, "A time came when, for a while, I was left with nothing on the physical plane. I had no relationships, no job, no home, no socially defined identity. I spent almost two years sitting on park benches in a state of the most intense joy" (2004: 5). Despite offering us a condensed and seemingly proven recipe to achieve enlightenment, Tolle concedes that not everyone will be able to achieve enlightenment, but there is a possibility that some people will. As he argues, "Throughout history, there have always been rare individuals who experienced a shift in consciousness and so realized within themselves that toward which all religions point. To describe that non-conceptual Truth, they then used the conceptual framework of their own religions" (Tolle 2005: 16).

Although not formally affiliated with any specific religion, one cannot help but notice various references in Tolle's writings to established spiritual traditions, especially Buddhism and Christianity. While Tolle's books only mention Daoism occasionally, as I illustrate below, the core message of his teachings closely resonates with a Daoist perspective on how humans can advance to higher levels of consciousness and enlightenment.

A Daoist Perception of Consciousness and Enlightenment

I will now briefly describe how consciousness and enlightenment are conceptualized in the Daoist classics of Laozi and Zhuangzi as analyzed by Toshihiko Izutsu (1984), the renowned 20th century scholar of comparative religion. Izutsu's extensive analysis of these two Daoist classical texts with regard to consciousness and enlightenment is summarized under five key points in Table 3.1. I will now elaborate on each of these points.

Oneness

The first important point in the Daoist view of consciousness is a belief in the oneness and unity of everything in the cosmos. As Izutsu notes, Laozi and Zhuangzi teach us that "all things *are* one eternally, beyond Time and Space" (Izutsu 1984: 316). While this may not be apparent to the average person who sees only multiplicity in the world, "in the eye of one who has experienced the Great Awakening, all things are One; all things *are* the Reality itself ... these 'things' are so many phenomenal forms of the absolute One. The 'unity of existence,' thus understood constitutes the very core of the philosophy of Lao-tzu and Chuang-tzu" (ibid.: 313). Izutsu describes this unity as "Being," stating that "the absolute One is of course the Way which pervades the whole world of Being; rather it *is* the whole world of Being. As such it transcends all distinctions and oppositions" (ibid.: 328). As Izutsu notes, according to Laozi and Zhuangzi, the Way (i.e. *Dao*) is all-pervading and "everywhere in the

Table 3.1 Daoist Perspective on Consciousness and Enlightenment

	Five Key Points in the Daoist Perspective
A.	Oneness: All in the cosmos is one, all are interconnected. Nothing is outside the one.
B.	Humans are Prisoners of Ego: Things from the material world alone are insufficient to bring contentment to humans and Ego makes us disconnected from Dao, the Source of all Being.
C.	Abandoning Ordinary Knowledge: Reconnecting with the Source of all Being requires relinquishing most socially conditioned beliefs and pursuits.
D.	Not Acting Independently of the Source: Our thoughts and behaviors should automatically flow from the Source and not go against the Source. We should be and let other things be as the Source has designed them to be.
E.	Unity/Reuniting with Dao/the Source of all Being is Enlightenment/Awakening and a necessary step to global transformation.

Source: Author's compilation based on his reading of Izutsu (1984), Laozi, and Zhuangzi.

world; the world itself *is* a self-manifestation of the Way" (ibid.: 336). There is nothing (including ourselves) that is outside this unity.

Humans as Prisoners of Ego

A second point Izutsu observes in Laozi and Zhuangzi is that the reason why people fail to experience fulfillment in this life is largely due to their ego/mind which makes them have boundless and insatiable desires. As Izutsu explains, "the mode of living of the common people goes against the natural course of things because they are at the mercy of Reason and common sense. Boundless desire and the argumentative Reason constitute the core of the 'ego.' And the 'ego' once formed goes on growing ever stronger until it dominates the whole existence of a man" (Izutsu 1984: 446–447). Humans suffer due to being prisoners of their egos as their egos usually have "supreme command" over them (ibid.: 447).

Using the term "mind" (心 *xin*) to represent the concept of "ego," Zhuangzi compares the pathological but all too common tendency of humans engaged in sitting-galloping (坐馳 *zuo chi*) with the rare but purifying activity of sitting-forgetting (坐忘 *zuo wang*): As Izutsu explains, the former refers to:

> The situation in which the mind of an ordinary person finds itself, in constant movement, going this way at this moment and that way at the next, in response to myriad impressions coming from outside to attract its attention to rouse its curiosity, never ceasing, to stop and rest for a moment, even then when the body is quietly seated. The body may be sitting still but the mind is running around. It is the human mind in such a state that the word *xin* (mind) designates in this context. It is the exact opposite of the mind in a state of calm peaceful concentration. It is easy to understand conceptually this opposition of the states of the mind, one "galloping around" and the other "sitting still and void" ... man himself is responsible for allowing the Mind to exercise such a tyrannical sway over him, for the tyranny of the Mind is nothing else than the tyranny of the "ego" – that false "ego" which, as we have seen above, he creates for himself as the ontological center of his personality ... The "ego," thus understood, is man's own creation. But man clings to it, as if it were something objective, even absolute. He can never imagine himself existing without it, and so he cannot abandon it for a moment.
>
> (Izutsu 1984: 333)

As this passage relates, Zhuangzi sees the ego/mind as "the source and origin of all human follies," on account of the mind's "unnatural rigidity" by which the mind's "distinguishing and discriminating ... perceives everywhere 'good' and 'bad,' 'right' and 'wrong' and regards these categories as something objective and absolute" (ibid.: 334). The problem that needs to be uprooted is our ordinary reasoning and thinking which is colored by biases that are a function of social conventions and socialization processes which are fundamentally out of step with the Way because the Way itself transcends all such conventions.

This tragedy of people being prisoners of their ego and hence disconnected from the Way is also particular to human beings who among the myriad creatures are uniquely out of step with the rest of nature:

> All things, whether inanimate or living, seem to exist or live in docile obedience to their own destinies. They seem to be happy and contented with existing in absolute conformity with the inevitable Law of Nature. They are, in this respect, naturally "living in accordance with the *tian li* (天理)." Only Man, of all existents, can and does revolt against the *tian li*. And that because of his self-consciousness. It is extremely difficult for him to be resigned to his destiny. He tends to struggle hard to evade it or to change it. And he thereby brings discordance into the universal harmony of Being. But of course all his violent struggles are vain and useless, for everything is determined externally. Herein lies the very source of the tragedy of human existence.
>
> (Izutsu 1984: 420–421)

Abandoning Distorted Knowledge

A third observation Izutsu finds at the core of Laozi's and Zhuangzi's philosophy is the need to abandon our ordinary distorted thoughts and knowledge in order to reach higher consciousness and enlightenment. This is necessary because true and deep knowledge of reality can only come to a person through direct unmediated transmission from *Dao* (the Way), the Source of all Creation. By contrast, much of the ordinary knowledge we acquire over the course of our lives is not that important or outright counter-productive for our spiritual development and for gaining a true understanding of reality and enlightenment. In stressing this point, Laozi and Zhuangzi expressed their objection to the traditional Confucian approach toward knowledge which placed strong emphasis on the elaborate learning of morals and manners – a view that was influential in their time. As Izutsu explains,

> By Learning (学 *xue*) is meant the study of the meticulous rules of conduct and behavior – concerning, for instance, on what occasions and to whom one should use the formal and polite expression "yes, sir" and when and to whom one should use the informal expression "hum!" – the kind of learning which was so strongly advocated by the Confucian school under the name of Ceremonies (礼 *li*).
>
> (Izutsu 1984: 329)

The kind of "knowing" which is wrong in the eyes of Lao-tzu is the same distinguishing and discriminating activity of intelligence as the one which we have seen is so bitterly denounced by Chuang-tzu. "Knowing" understood in this sense, is denounced because it disturbs the minds of the people in an unnecessary and wrong way. And the disturbance of the mind by the perception of values, positive and negative, is regarded by Lao-tzu as wrong and detrimental to human existence because it tempts it away from its real nature, and ultimately from the Way itself.

(Izutsu 1984: 335)

As discussed in the passages above, it is the evaluational aspect of knowing that is most problematic. What is particularly damaging and dangerous is that we label things as good or bad and as right or wrong, instead of just accepting them as they are. Laozi and Zhuangzi condemn such rigidity and judge-mentalism. Instead, they teach us the importance of "forgetting about passing judgments, whether implicit or explicit, on anything. One should, Chuang-tzu emphasizes, put oneself in a mental state prior to all judgments, prior to all activity of Reason, in which one would see things in their original – or 'Heavenly' as he says 'essence-less state'" (Izutsu 1984: 325). The method Zhuangzi recommends to reach a mental state prior to all judgments is through "fasting of the mind" (心斋 *xin zhai*) by which man lets go of his thoughts to become "ego-less" and be "one with the 'ten thousand things'; he *becomes* the 'ten thousand things' … A complete and perfect harmony is here realized between the 'interior' and the 'exterior'; there is no distinction between them" (Izutsu 1984: 345).

Not Acting Independently of the Source

A fourth point noted by Izutsu in the Daoist classics is that our actions (and not only our state of mind) should be in tune with and emanate from the Way. This means we should neither depart from nor act independently of the Source of all life and creativity. Aligning our actions with the Source is termed *wuwei* (無爲), often translated as "non-doing." As Izutsu explains, "'Non-Doing' means, in short, man's abandoning all artificial, unnatural effort to do something, and [instead] identifying himself completely with the activity of Nature which is nothing other than the spontaneous self-manifestation of the Way itself" (Izutsu 1984: 309). He explains this as follows:

Everything is necessarily fixed and determined by a kind of Cosmic Will which is called the Command or Heaven. As long as there is even the minutest discrepancy in the consciousness of a man between this Cosmic

Will and his own personal will, Necessity is felt to be something forced upon him, something which he has to accept even against his will. If, under such conditions, through resignation he gains "freedom" to some extent, it cannot be a complete freedom. Complete freedom is obtained only when man identifies himself with Necessity itself, that is, the natural course of things and events, and goes on transforming himself as the natural course of things turns this way or that.

(Izutsu 1984: 423)

As indicated in the excerpt above, being one with the Way enables us to go along with the nature of things. True freedom is thus just to go with the flow. However, until we overcome our ego, we will tend to resist the nature of things and find ourselves running faster and faster in a vicious cycle on a hedonic treadmill. Contrastingly, Daoism accepts, encourages, and lets things "be as they are" – also known as *ziran* (自然). *Ziran* is the nature of Dao as emphasized in Laozi chapter 25.

Reuniting with the Source as Enlightenment

The fifth and seemingly most important element in Izutsu's analysis of the Daoist classics is that reuniting with the Dao, the Source of all Life, is Enlightenment, the highest, most fulfilling experience a person can ever have. As Izutsu explains, "Lao-tzu talks about *sheng ren* (聖人) or the 'sacred man' ... a man who has attained to the highest stage of the intuition of the Way, to the extent of being completely unified with it, and who behaves accordingly in this world following the dictates of the Way that he feels active in himself. He is, in brief, a human embodiment of the Way" (Izutsu 1984: 301). What distinguishes the enlightened sage or "sacred man" in Daoism from ordinary people is that through personal spiritual cultivation methods like sitting-forgetting and mind-fasting:

The **"ego" is thereby completely destroyed**, and the world, both external and internal, disappears from the consciousness. And as the "ego" is nullified, the inner eye of the man is opened and the light of "illumination" suddenly breaks through the darkness of spiritual night. This marks the birth of a new Ego in man. **He now finds himself in the Eternal Now, beyond all limitation of time and space**. He is also "beyond Life and Death," that is, **he is "one" with all things, and all things are unified into "one"** in his "no-consciousness." **In this spiritual state, an unusual Tranquility or Calmness reigns over everything**. And in this cosmic Tranquility, away from the turmoil and agitation of the sensible world, man enjoys being unified and identified with the very process of the universal Transformation of the ten thousand things.

(Izutsu 1984: 476, bold added)

As for the outward manifestation of the enlightened person:

> The man himself is no longer involved in the hustle and bustle of incessantly changing phenomena. The man at this stage is a calm observer of things, and his mind is like a polished mirror. He accepts everything as it comes into his "interior," and sees it off, unperturbed, as it goes out of sight. There is for him nothing to be rejected, but there is nothing willfully to be pursued either. He is, in short, beyond "good" and "bad," "right" and "wrong."
>
> (Izutsu 1984: 345)

To reiterate, in the enlightened state, one is not bothered by anything. One experiences pure tranquility and bliss and "having no ego, he adapts himself to everything and every event with limitless flexibility" (Izutsu 1984: 441). In interactions with others, the sacred person/sage becomes a model of goodness and s/he supports the myriad beings to be who they naturally are instead of scheming to use them for his/her own selfish purposes. As Izutsu explains,

> Since everything is himself as he goes on transforming himself with the cosmic Transmutation – he accepts willingly and lovingly whatever happens to him or whatever he observes.
>
> (Izutsu 1984: 425)

> He finds everything good – early death is good, old age is good, the beginning is good, the end is good ... And yet he serves as a model for the people in this respect. All the more so, then, should (the Way itself be taken as the model for all men – the Way) upon which depend the ten thousand things and which is the very ground of the universal Transmutation.
>
> (Izutsu 1984: 426)

> The "sacred man" ... only helps the "being-so-of-itself" (i.e., spontaneous being) of the ten thousand things.
>
> (Izutsu 1984: 403)

To conclude, in Izutsu's analysis of consciousness and enlightenment in the Daoist classics of Laozi and Zhuangzi, we find five main points and much use of the terms Being, Ego, Knowledge, Unity of Existence, Enlightenment, and (Eternal) Now. As will now be explored, Eckhart Tolle uses almost identical terms and language to explain his (own) views on consciousness and enlightenment.

Eckhart Tolle's Perception of Consciousness and Enlightenment

Oneness

As in Daoism, Eckhart Tolle contends that everything in the world is interconnected and ultimately one. While Daoism uses the words Dao (Way) (道 *dao*)
or One (一 *yi*) to describe this unity and oneness of all things, Tolle employs
the terms "Being" or alternatively "God" or "One Life." As Tolle states,

> Underneath the surface appearance, everything is not only connected with
> everything else, but also with the Source of all life out of which it came.
>
> (Tolle 2005: 25)

> What is God? The eternal One Life underneath all the forms of life. What
> is love? To feel the presence of that One Life deep within yourself and
> within all creatures. To be it. Therefore, all love is the love of God.
>
> (Tolle 2004: 155)

> God is Being itself, not a being. There can be no subject-object relation-
> ship here, no duality, no you *and* God. God-realization is the most natural
> thing there is. The amazing and incomprehensible fact is not that you *can*
> become conscious of God but that you are *not* conscious of God.
>
> (Tolle 2004: 224)

> Since time immemorial, flowers, crystals, precious stones, and birds have held
> special significance for the human spirit. Like all life-forms, they are, of course,
> temporary manifestations of the underlying one Life, one Consciousness.
>
> (Tolle 2005: 4)

In the Daoist conception of existence, all in the world are one, and this
unity includes both emptiness/nothingness (*wu* 無) and things/being (*you* 有).
Tolle (2005: 217) similarly claims the universe consists of both things and
nothing, and these two components together comprise reality:

> Here are the two dimensions that make up reality, thing-ness and no-thing-
> ness, form and the denial of form, which is the recognition that form is not
> who you are.
>
> (ibid.: 221)

> Physicists have discovered that the apparent solidity of matter is an il-
> lusion created by our senses. This includes the physical body, which we
> perceive and think of as form, but 99.99% of which is actually space.
>
> (ibid.: 250)

So your physical body, which is form, reveals itself as essentially formless when you go deeper into it. It becomes a doorway into inner space. Although inner space has no form, it is intensely alive. That "empty space" is life in its fullness, the un-manifested Source out of which all manifestation flows. The traditional word for that Source is God.

(ibid.: 251)

Tolle references the Daoist sage Laozi on this point regarding how "Space comes into being the moment the One becomes two, and as 'two' become the 'ten thousand things,' as Lao Tse calls the manifested world, space becomes more and more vast" (Tolle 2004: 140).

In the same way that Daoism emphasizes the all-pervasive and all-encompassing "Dao," Tolle sees everything united in "Being." As Tolle asserts, "I prefer to call it Being. Being is prior to existence. Existence is form, content, 'what happens.' Existence is the foreground of life; Being is the background, as it were" (2005: 220). For Tolle, Being was present before being separated into form (existence) and form-less (space/nothing-ness) which is identical to the teachings of Laozi in Chapter 1 of the Daodejing (道德经) which states that both nothingness (form-less) and existence (form) spring from the same root (the *Dao*) – the former being the origin of heaven and earth while the latter is the mother of the 10,000 things (all life forms). Daoists use the term "*Dao*" (Way) to refer to the "Source" of all life while also recognizing that it ultimately has no name as it transcends human language and understanding. Tolle likewise sees the one true Source as ineffable and beyond human understanding. As he notes, no words and "no thought can encapsulate the vastness of the totality" (ibid.: 280).

Humans as Prisoners of Ego

As in Daoism, Eckhart Tolle maintains that we humans will never experience contentment, awakening, or enlightenment as long as we seek well-being from material things and the material world. As with classical Daoists, Tolle also believes the fundamental problem we need to overcome is that our psyche is controlled by the ego and its fear of annihilation/death and this ruins almost everything in our lives (Tolle 2004: 44). Tragically, people tend to always feel incomplete and "often enter into a compulsive pursuit of ego-gratification and things to identify with in order to fill this hole they feel within. So they strive after possessions, money, success, power, recognition, or a special relationship, basically so that they can feel better about themselves, feel more complete. But even when they attain all these things, they soon find that the hole is still there, that it is bottomless" (2004: 45). The underlying problem, in Tolle's diagnosis, is a false consciousness plaguing most humans that makes our dissatisfaction unable to go away. As Tolle explains,

> As long as the egoic mind is running your life, you cannot truly be at ease; you cannot be at peace or fulfilled except for brief intervals when you obtained what you wanted, when a craving has just been fulfilled.
>
> (Tolle 2004: 46)

> Those who have not found their true wealth, which is the radiant joy of Being and the deep, unshakable peace that comes with it are beggars, even if they have great material wealth. They are looking outside for scraps of pleasure or fulfillment, for validation, security, or love, while they have a treasure within that not only includes all those things but is infinitely greater than anything the world can offer.
>
> (Tolle 2004: 12)

Tolle also agrees with the Daoist view that seeking fulfillment only through material things means chasing after illusions. Tolle sees this malady as both an individual and a social dysfunction. Here again Tolle and Daoism converge in their critique of the unhealthiness of many of society's ways and tendencies. As Tolle laments,

> Paradoxically, what keeps the so-called consumer society going is the fact that trying to find yourself through things doesn't work: The ego satisfaction is short-lived and so you keep looking for more, keep buying, keep consuming.
>
> (Tolle 2005: 36)

> Unease, restlessness, boredom, anxiety, dissatisfaction, are the result of unfulfilled wanting. Wanting is structural, so no amount of content can provide lasting fulfillment as long as that mental structure remains in place.
>
> (Tolle 2005: 47)

As in Daoism, Tolle sees both individual human beings and human societies as having an overwhelming tendency to apply superficial and ineffective remedies to address their problems instead of going to the fundamental root cause and uprooting the underlying disease. As Tolle (2004: 222) notes, "there are many pseudo escapes – work, drink, drugs, anger, projection, suppression, and so on – but they don't free you from the pain." The root problem in his view is being estranged and disconnected from Being, the Source, the One, or as Daoists call it, the *Dao*. According to Tolle,

> The "normal" state of mind of most human beings contains a strong element of what we might call dysfunction or even madness.
>
> (Tolle 2005: 8)

Humans have been in the grip of pain for eons, ever since they fell from the state of grace, entered the realm of time and mind, and lost awareness of Being. At that point, they started to perceive themselves as meaningless fragments in an alien universe, unconnected to the Source and to each other.

(Tolle 2004: 31)

Anyone who is identified with their mind and, therefore, disconnected from their true power, their deeper self rooted in Being, will have fear as their constant companion.

(Tolle 2004: 45)

A great irony in all of this is that Being (the *Dao*) is all around us, but most people fail to take notice of it. Yet, the price we pay for being disconnected to the Source is immense:

The physical needs for food, water, shelter, clothing, and basic comforts could be easily met for all humans on the planet, were it not for the imbalance of resources created by the insane and rapacious need for more, the greed of the ego. It finds collective expression in the economic structures of this world, such as the huge corporations, which are egoic entities that compete with each other for more. Their only blind aim is profit. They pursue that aim with absolute ruthlessness. Nature, animals, people, even their own employees, are no more than digits on a balance sheet, lifeless objects to be used, then discarded.

(Tolle 2005: 48)

The human ego in its collective aspect as "us" against "them" is even more insane than the "me," the individual ego, although the mechanism is the same ... Greed, selfishness, exploitation, cruelty, and violence are still all-pervasive ... as individual and collective manifestations of an underlying dysfunction or mental illness.

(Tolle 2005: 73)

Many types of illness are caused by the ego's continuous resistance, which creates restrictions and blockages in the flow of energy through the body. When you reconnect with Being and are no longer run by your mind, you cease to create those things. You do not create or participate in drama anymore.

(Tolle 2004: 181)

As Tolle indicates, due to our ego's continuous resistance, we experience unrelenting physical and mental pain on account of our disconnectedness from Being (the Source) and not being fully in the Present. This ego-driven suffering is the opposite of Daoist *yangsheng* (nourishing life; see Chapter 2) and especially harms women and nature:

> We now have a situation in which the suppression of the feminine has become internalized, even in most women. The sacred feminine, because it is suppressed, is felt by many women as emotional pain.
>
> (Tolle 2005: 157)

> The ego can take root and grow more easily in the male form than in the female. This is because women are less mind-identified than men. They are more in touch with the inner body and the intelligence of the organism where the intuitive faculties originate. The female form ... has greater openness and sensitivity toward other life-forms, and is more attuned to the natural world. If the balance between male and female energies had not been destroyed on our planet, the ego's growth would have been greatly curtailed. We would not have declared war on nature, and we would not be so completely alienated from our Being.
>
> (Tolle 2005: 155)

The idea that women and females are closer and more attuned to the natural world than males is also a theme that appears in Laozi who deplores the subjugation and subordination of women and female energies in the world (Joshi 2023).

As can be seen from the quotes above, in Tolle's view, because of our false consciousness, ego-attachment, and disconnectedness from the Source, we blame others for our dissatisfaction and frustrations. Along the way, we bring a lot of harm to ourselves and to others although we typically remain oblivious to much of the harm that we cause. There is a very strong overlap here between Tolle's teachings and the Daoist classics. Both see ego attachment as a root cause of much of our suffering and our disconnectedness from the One.

Abandoning Distorted Knowledge

As with Laozi and Zhuangzi, Tolle's books teach us that in order to relinquish our ego and return to the One, we must abandon ordinary knowledge and become fully in the present, fully aware, fully in sync with Being, fully alive. Resembling the Daoist critique of ordinary knowledge, Tolle asserts that our minds have been colonized and conditioned in unhealthy ways. As a result, we are holders of distorted knowledge, unable to see the truth, and this prevents us from truly experiencing the fullness of Being. Although we are unaware of many of the thoughts in our mind and their detrimental effects, these thoughts obstruct us from perceiving true reality. Similarly, Zhuangzi hinted that our life is like a dream. Until we realize the damage our thoughts do we remain prisoners of our mind. As Tolle explains,

> Nothing is what it seems to be ... whatever you perceive is only a kind of symbol, like an image in a dream ... An infinite number of completely different interpretations, completely different worlds, is possible and, in fact, exists – all depending on the perceiving consciousness.
>
> (Tolle 2004: 199)

> Choice begins the moment you dis-identify from the mind and its conditioned patterns, the moment you become present. Until you reach that point, you are unconscious, spiritually speaking. This means that you are compelled to think, feel, and act in certain ways according to the conditioning of your mind.
>
> (Tolle 2004: 226)

> Identification with your mind creates an opaque screen of concepts, labels, images, words, judgments, and definitions that blocks all true relationship. It comes between you and yourself, between you and your fellow man and woman, between you and nature, between you and God. It is this screen of thought that creates the illusion of separateness, the illusion that there is you *and* a totally separate "other." You then forget the essential fact that, underneath the level of physical appearances and separate forms, you are one with all that *is*.
>
> (Tolle 2004: 15)

> When you don't cover up the world with words and labels, a sense of the miraculous returns to your life that was lost a long time ago when humanity, instead of using thought, became possessed by thought. A depth returns to your life ... The quicker you are in attaching verbal or mental labels to things, people, or situations, the more shallow and lifeless your reality becomes, and the more deadened you become to reality ... Words reduce reality to something the human mind can grasp, which isn't very much.
>
> (Tolle 2005: 26)

Like the Daoist emphasis on the inability of words to communicate thoughts as taught by Laozi and Zhuangzi, Tolle sees words and labels as distorting our consciousness and thereby masking the true underlying reality.[2]

Resembling classical Daoists, in Tolle's view, about 80%–90% of people's thinking is useless or harmful, and the negativity which we typically feel in our lives is always counterproductive (Tolle 2004: 22). What he recommends instead is to "dis-identify from your mind" (ibid.: 21) in order to get to the state of "no-mind," the term he uses to refer to "consciousness without thought ... Only in that way is it possible to think creatively ... All true artists, whether they know it or not, create from a place of no-mind, from inner still-ness. The mind then gives form to the creative impulse or insight" (ibid.: 24).

As our comparative analysis reveals, Tolle condemns the pathology of ego and exposes the limits of language to communicate between people and to get at the oneness of the world. Resembling the parables of Zhuangzi, Tolle asserts that we should eschew rigidity in our thinking and not be closed to al-ternative interpretations of reality (Tolle 2005: 19). Tolle contends that "when you fully accept that you don't know, you actually enter a state of peace and clarity that is closer to who you truly are than thought could ever be" (Tolle 2005: 90). This mirrors Laozi chapter 71 which states that "to know that one does not know is best; Not to know but to believe that one knows is a disease. Only by seeing this disease as a disease can one be free of it. Sages are free of this disease; Because they see this disease as a disease, they are free of it."

Not Acting Independently of the Source

In Eckhart Tolle's view, we can all significantly improve our lives by stop-ping our constant thinking about the past and the future and instead just live fully in this moment. In this way, we can also experience great freedom by simply accepting what actually is (instead of being delusional or naïve) and to work with it instead of against it. In his teachings, he emphasizes that "nonresistance, nonjudgment, and nonattachment are the three aspects of true freedom and enlightened living" (Tolle 2005: 225). As Tolle states, "allow the present moment to be" in order to experience "the state of true inner peace. Then see what happens, and take action if necessary or possi-ble. Accept – then act. Whatever the present moment contains, accept it as if you had chosen it. Always work with it, not against it. Make it your friend and ally, not your enemy. This will miraculously transform your whole life" (Tolle 2004: 35).

Tolle's recommendation for how we should act when confronting a situa-tion also resembles the Daoist prescription of *wuwei* as discussed above. As Tolle notes, "sometimes letting things go is an act of far greater power than defending or hanging on" (Tolle 2005: 41). Like Daoist *wuwei*, the important thing for us is to act "out of present-moment awareness" rather than out of "a reaction coming from the past conditioning of your mind" (Tolle 2004: 66). When we do something, our actions should emerge as "an intuitive response to the situation" which means that at times we will "find it more effective to do nothing" (ibid.: 66). Tolle even mentions the Daoist concept of *wuwei* to make this key point:

> Nonresistance doesn't necessarily mean doing nothing. All it means is that any "doing" becomes nonreactive ... Having said that "doing noth-ing" when you are in a state of intense presence is a very powerful transformer and healer of situations and people. In Taoism, there is a

term called *wuwei*, which is usually translated as "action-less activity" or "sitting quietly doing nothing." In ancient China, this was regarded as one of the highest achievements or virtues. It is radically different from inactivity in the ordinary state of consciousness, or rather unconsciousness, which stems from fear, inertia, or indecision. The real "doing nothing" implies inner nonresistance and intense alertness. On the other hand, if action is required, you will no longer react from your conditioned mind, but you will respond to the situation out of your conscious presence.

(Tolle 2004: 215–216)

For Tolle, the practice of *wuwei* is a means of surrendering oneself fully to Being in line with the great emphasis Laozi places on yielding when facing an adversary in order to avoid unnecessary inter-personal or inter-state conflict (Joshi 2024b). As Tolle notes,

Surrender is the simple but profound wisdom of *yielding* to rather than *opposing* the flow of life. The only place where you can experience the flow of life is the Now, so to surrender is to accept the present moment unconditionally and without reservation. It is to relinquish inner resistance to what *is*.

(Tolle 2004: 205)

When you yield internally, when you surrender, a new dimension of consciousness opens up. If action is possible or necessary, your action will be in alignment with the whole and supported by creative intelligence, the unconditioned consciousness which in a state of inner openness you become one with. Circumstances and people then become helpful, cooperative. Coincidences happen. If no action is possible, you rest in the peace and inner stillness that come with surrender.

(Tolle 2005: 57)

Surrender is perfectly compatible with taking action, initiating change, or achieving goals. But in the surrendered state a totally different energy, a different quality, flows into your doing. Surrender reconnects you with the source-energy of Being, and if your doing is infused with Being, it becomes a joyful celebration of life energy that takes you more deeply into the Now ... We could call this "*surrendered action*."

(Tolle 2004: 208)

Resembling the Daoists, Tolle likewise sees the human body as an energy field. Like the Daoist concept of *qi* and the practices of *qigong* and *taijiquan* (a.k.a. t'ai-chi) which were discussed in Chapter 2, Tolle extolls "the free flow of life energy through the body, which is essential for its healthy functioning" (Tolle 2004: 207). Tolle favors embracing and developing the body's energies to live more naturally and to facilitate higher consciousness and enlightenment:

> Every human being emanates an energy field that corresponds to his or her inner state, and most people can sense it, although they may feel someone else's energy emanation only subliminally. That is to say, they don't know that they sense it, yet it determines to a large extent how they feel about and react to that person.
>
> (Tolle 2005: 162)

> [The] practice of t'ai chi ... this movement meditation that stills the mind. This makes a considerable difference to the collective energy field and goes some way toward diminishing the pain-body by reducing thinking and generating Presence ... Spiritual practices that involve the physical body, such as t'ai chi, qigong, and yoga ... will play an important role in the global awakening.
>
> (Tolle 2005: 158–159)

Reuniting with the Source as Enlightenment

On all four of the previous points, Tolle's conception of consciousness closely resembles that of Daoism. In Tolle's narrative, if we cease our compulsive thinking and completely focus on our breath, we can reunite with the One. As he quips, "Be aware of your breathing as often as you are able, whenever you remember. Do that for one year, and it will be more powerfully transformative than attending all of these [self-improvement] courses. And it's free" (2005: 244). As Tolle explains,

> Being aware of your breath forces you into the present moment – the key to all inner transformations. Whenever you are conscious of the breath, you are absolutely present. You may also notice that you cannot think *and* be aware of your breathing. Conscious breathing stops your mind. But far from being in a trance or half asleep, you are fully awake and highly alert. You are not falling below thinking, but rising above it. And if you look more closely, you will find that those two things – coming fully into the present moment and ceasing thinking without loss of consciousness – are actually one and the same.
>
> (Tolle 2005: 246)

Engaging in the practice of conscious breathing can enable us to reunite with Being, the Source (*Dao*), and through this unity we can then experience *enlightenment* which Tolle describes as "a realm of deep stillness and peace, but also of joy and intense aliveness" (Tolle 2004: 130):

> The word enlightenment conjures up the idea of some super human accomplishment, and the ego likes to keep it that way, but it is simply your natural state of *felt* oneness with Being. It is a state of connectedness with something immeasurable and indestructible, something that, almost paradoxically, is essentially you and yet is much greater than you. It is finding your true nature beyond name and form.
>
> (Tolle 2004: 12)

> The whole is made up of existence and Being, the manifested and the un-manifested, the world and God. So when you become aligned with the whole, you become a conscious part of the interconnectedness of the whole and its purpose: the emergence of consciousness into this world. As a result, spontaneous helpful occurrences, chance encounters, coincidences, and synchronistic events happen much more frequently.
>
> (Tolle 2005: 277)

> You become a bridge between the Unmanifested and the manifested, between God and the world. This is the state of connectedness with the Source that we call enlightenment.
>
> (Tolle 2004: 132)

Lastly, the idea in Tolle's teachings that the person who has transcended the world can bring about a better world resembles Laozi's teachings about the Daoist sage. Yet, somewhat paradoxically in both Tolle's writings and in Daoism, the enlightened sage is humble and relatively obscure. As Tolle notes, resembling the parables of Zhuangzi, a number of ordinary people may even be enlightened to a certain degree as reflected in their being unburdened by ego and one with what they do. For the person who is enlightened,

> You can still enjoy the passing pleasures of this world, but there is no fear of loss anymore, so you don't need to cling to them. Although you can enjoy sensory pleasures, the craving for sensory experience is gone, as is the constant search for fulfillment through psychological gratification, through feeding the ego. You are in touch with something infinitely greater than any pleasure, greater than any manifested thing … In a way, you then don't need the world anymore. You don't even need it to be different from the way it is. It is only at this point that you begin to make a real contribution toward bringing about a better world, toward creating a different order of

reality. It is only at this point that you are able to feel true compassion and to help others at the level of cause. Only those who have transcended the world can bring about a better world.

(Tolle 2004: 201)

Conclusion

As illustrated in this chapter, Eckhart Tolle's new age teachings on consciousness and enlightenment are very similar to what is taught in the Daoist classics of Laozi and Zhuangzi and can even be seen as largely a restatement of traditional Daoist teachings for a contemporary audience. Tolle, like Daoists, emphasizes the five key points mentioned above as identified by Izutsu and Tolle likewise endorses the emancipatory roles of breathing and meditation, abandoning ego and excessive thinking, and relinquishing ordinary, distorted, evaluative knowledge.

There are of course naturally some discrepancies between Daoist thought and Tolle's teachings as one would find between any two thinkers or spiritual traditions. One difference is that Tolle pays less attention to the role of the body in nourishing life (养生 *yangsheng*) compared to Daoism. But this is also a matter of degree. Tolle is not inattentive to this route to spiritual cultivation and does mention the body as reservoir of energy stating that "transformation is *through* the body, not away from it" (Tolle 2004: 114). Unlike Laozi and Zhuangzi, Tolle also invokes a notion of karma and rebirth. As Tolle contends, when we die, we just move on and our consciousness "reincarnates into another form" (Tolle 2005: 292). Tolle also comes across as an idealist (or conceptualist) as opposed to a realist. For instance, he states: "Remember that your perception of the world is a reflection of your state of consciousness. You are not separate from it, and there is no objective world out there. Every moment, your consciousness creates the world that you inhabit" (Tolle 2004: 198). The Daoist classics do not appear to take a definitive stand one way or the other as to whether there is an objective world out there as it seems to be beside the point for them. Thus, not all of Tolle's teachings can be categorized as Daoist. But as demonstrated here, on essential points concerning the nature of consciousness and enlightenment, there is a significant overlap suggesting that Tolle, Laozi, and Zhuangzi might have all been tapping into the same source, set of ideas, or perhaps even universal consciousness.

To conclude, Daoist ideas about consciousness and enlightenment are clearly echoed in the books of one of the most influential new spiritual teachers of the past half-century. These teachings are not only potentially valuable for individuals today seeking to improve their well-being and spiritual development but might also benefit the rest of society as well. This guidance for aiding individuals and society is precisely what the Daoist tradition has been teaching for generations, and their new articulation via Tolle's writings has helped to spread such awareness internationally to contemporary societies struggling with the underlying problem (and myriad symptoms) of human attachment to ego/mind. The correspondence between Daoism and Tolle's new age teachings also reveals what appears to be increasing cross-cultural receptivity to an important dimension of Daoist thought in the new millennium showing that Daoism's global influence today is probably much greater than generally perceived.

Notes

1 Author's observation at the 17th International Conference of Daoist Studies held in Taichung, Taiwan.
2 As in the Daoist classics, Tolle defends a mystical epistemology and claims his awareness about consciousness "is not derived from external sources, but from the one true Source" (2004: 10).

4 The Ethics of a Daoist Sage
Lessons from the *Wenzi*

Introduction

Daoist (a.k.a. Taoist) thought maintains that individuals and societies have lost their way by falling into a tragic state of disconnectedness from the Way (*Dao*), the source of all life and creativity. What the Daoist classics tell us is that deviating from the Way, the generative source of everything in the universe, is the primary source of our individual discontent and collective problems as discussed in Chapter 3. Hence, Daoists have regularly expressed strong dissent against how so many ruling (political, economic, and social/cultural) elites have deviated from the Way.

In response to this tragedy, a powerful solution offered by Daoists relies on the role of sages who are uniquely positioned (due to already being in harmony with the Way) to bring society (more) in line with the Way. These unique people live peaceful, contented lives and possess a special ability to potentially help return the whole world to a state of great peace. But what exactly is the ethical character of a Daoist sage? How do we recognize a sage? A short answer to these questions is that the Daoist classics differ on this point with the Laozi envisioning a relatively altruistic sage who works to benefit all in the community, whereas in the Zhuangzi, we find a more escapist sage who focuses mostly on his own personal cultivation instead of getting too involved in worldly affairs. Compiled several hundred years later than the transmitted texts of Laozi and Zhuangzi, the *Wenzi* (a.k.a. Wen-tzu) helpfully offers us an even more developed and detailed picture of the Daoist sage's life.

Although less studied compared to Laozi's *Daodejing* (DDJ) (a.k.a. *Tao Te Ching*) or the Zhuangzi (a.k.a. Chuang-tzu), the *Wenzi* has long been seen as a great Daoist classic (e.g. Cleary 1992; Van Els 2018). The received edition of *Wenzi* was likely compiled between the third and fifth centuries CE though much of its content predates this period by several centuries (Van Els 2018).[1] The *Wenzi* text itself is an anthology featuring an assortment of wisdom among its various 180 sub-sections which (like the 81 chapters of Laozi) have no particularly obvious method of organization (Van Els 2018: 188). The *Wenzi* also draws upon several different original sources including the *Huainanzi*

DOI: 10.4324/9781003517344-4

(a.k.a. *Huainan-tzu*) text (originating from the second century BCE) and a first-century BCE "proto-Wenzi" text discovered on bamboo strips in the 1970s during an ancient tomb excavation (Van Els 2014; Fech 2015, 2018).[2]

At the peak of its influence, the *Wenzi* text was given imperial recognition and the honorific title of *Tongxuan Zhenjing* (通玄真经) or "Authentic Scripture of Pervading Mystery" during China's Tang dynasty (618–905 CE) when it became one of four Daoist classics tested in state civil service examinations (Sakade 2008: 1041).[3] As Van Els (2018: 159) notes, from the third century CE to the mid-12th century, there was widespread circulation of and reverence for the *Wenzi* as a valuable source of quotations before being later perceived as "inauthentic" and subsequently largely neglected from the 13th century until the 1970s re-discovery of the proto-*Wenzi*.

In this chapter, I look to the *Wenzi* for guidance in understanding the ethical characteristics of the Daoist sage. The *Wenzi* has played an important role in the Daoist tradition, and it touches upon a variety of themes from the ethical and the political to the spiritual and the metaphysical. Mirroring other Daoist classics, the sage plays a prominent role in the text, and although depicted in a variety of ways throughout the *Wenzi*, there are certain common threads in those depictions.

The Ethics of a Daoist Sage

As I will now explain, the following eight ethical principles appear repeatedly in the *Wenzi* as important attributes of a Daoist sage: humility, relative obscurity, tranquility, sincerity, meditation, impartiality, loving-kindness, and simplicity/emptiness.

Humility

A first key principle of the sage is humility. As described by the *Wenzi*, this involves neither bragging nor boasting about one's knowledge, one's good deeds, or one's spiritual accomplishments. Practicing humility means neither putting other people down nor indirectly communicating one's superiority over others in any sort of way. It suggests a general orientation toward not talking too much – allocating a much greater share of time to listening and to silence than to speaking. In addition to humility impacting what we say and refrain from saying, the *Wenzi*'s conception of humility implies being willing to calmly, unresentfully, and un-begrudgingly accept low status in the world and a willingness to accept the lowest positions within social organizations (such as at one's workplace, religious community, school, etc.), in social groups (such as amongst friends or family members), and in society at large. This willingness to accept low status occurs despite the sage's abilities and accomplishments – attainments and awareness that may very well be at a significantly higher level than others around them.

A key to achieving such humility is detaching from one's ego and not comparing oneself to others. Instead, one completely focuses their attention on one's own immeasurably inferior capabilities and status vis-à-vis the great *Dao* of the universe, the source of all life and the myriad things. As one becomes humble vis-à-vis the Dao, it then becomes possible to learn and put into practice the wisdom of being humble vis-à-vis everyone else and everything else in the universe. Fundamentally, re-orienting one's mindset in this way enables us to follow nature spontaneously. This, in turn, enables great things to happen. As the *Wenzi* explains,

A gigantic tree begins as a sprout, a huge building starts at the bottom. This is the Way of Nature. Sages emulate this, lowering themselves with humility, withdrawing to put themselves last, minimizing themselves by frugality, and lessening themselves by detachment ... by being lesser they become great.

(Wenzi §72)[4]

Sages do not seek renown for their acts and do not seek praise for their knowledge. Their management follows nature spontaneously, without them adding anything themselves.

(Wenzi §54)

The sage kings of ancient times spoke humbly to others and placed themselves after others.

(Wenzi §67)

One might wonder whether the humility of sages and sage-kings as mentioned in the passages above is truly genuine or merely contrived – is it real or just (symbolically) for show? The answer the *Wenzi* text provides is that it should be thoroughly genuine. One ought to free oneself of all conceit, thoroughly listen to others, and the higher one's position is, the more humble one should be. As the *Wenzi* declares:

Ancient kings presided over the land by means of the Way ... They lived in the midst of great fulfillment yet were not extravagant; they were in high and noble positions yet were not arrogant.

(Wenzi §78)

Those who attain the Way are weak in ambition but strong at work, their minds are open and their responses are fitting ... Tranquil and uncontrived, when they act they do not miss the timing. Therefore nobility must be rooted in humility.

(Wenzi §9)

Ideal people do not put on an outward show of humanity and justice, but inwardly they cultivate the virtues of the Way.

(Wenzi §56)

When rulers are humble to their subjects they are lucid and clear, and when they are not humble to their subjects they are blind and deaf.

(Wenzi §95)

As seen in these excerpts, the ideal person does not put on an outward show of their greatness and morality. Neither extravagant nor arrogant, they are uncontrived and humble to all.

The opposite of sagely humility is actively pursuing a public reputation and seeking praise for being good and for doing good deeds. The *Wenzi* criticizes such behavior for it is likely to bring misfortune:

Those who wish to command a reputation … abandon the public and take to the private. Turning their backs on the Way, they take things upon themselves; they do good when they see they will be praised for it, setting themselves up as worthies. Under these conditions, government does not accord with reason.

(Wenzi §44)

People have three resentments. Those whose status is high are envied by others. Those whose offices are important are hated by the rulers. Those whose income is large are resented by others. So the higher the status, the humbler one should be, the greater the office, the more careful one should be, and the larger the income, the more generous one should be. Those who exercise these three things are not resented. Therefore nobility is based on lowliness, elevation is founded on humility.

(Wenzi §63)

Gather people by humility, win them by generosity; preserve yourself by restraint, and do not dare to be complacent. If you are not humble, people will become estranged and alienated. If you do not nurture them, the people will be rebellious.

(Wenzi §84)

As these passages indicate, in addition to possible spiritual motivations for pursuing sagely ethics such as salvation in the afterlife, there are also practical reasons to be humble and to adopt an ethics of humility. Namely, by exercising humility, one can preclude resentment, alienation, animosity, and rebellion.

Relative Obscurity

In line with humility, a second ethical principle of Daoist sages found in the *Wenzi* can be labeled "relative obscurity." In the same way that *Dao* is relatively obscure (i.e. not noticed by most) but still benevolent, sages are like this too. Sages are not necessarily totally hidden from public view. Rather, the important point is that they restrain themselves in their actions, and they refrain from being in and seeking out the limelight. Sages do not pursue fame or reputation. Nor do they seek popularity, notoriety, or having much in the way of possessions or profits. What sages succeed in doing is just getting the necessary work done without seeking attention or praise for it. This is precisely the way of the great *Dao* of the cosmos, the source of all life and creativity, even though most people fail to discern this or to appreciate it. As the *Wenzi* explains,

> The natural constant Way gives birth to beings but does not possess them, it produces evolution but does not rule it ... It is so ungraspable and undefinable that it cannot be imagined.
>
> (Wenzi §2)

> The Way molds myriad beings but is ever formless. Silent and unmoving, it totally comprehends the undifferentiated unknown ... It has no house but gives birth to all the names of the existent and nonexistent.
>
> (Wenzi §4)

Like the unobservable *Dao* that gives life to all things, sages nurture life while avoiding public recognition and accolades.

At the same time, it is worth noting that the Way (*Dao*) is not so obscure that no one ever finds it. Some seekers and non-seekers do in fact discover the Way. It is just that the Way is relatively obscure and always humble. Resembling the Way, sages give selflessly without seeking to get praise in return. As a result, many people do not even notice or appreciate the benevolence of sages because sages try to stay out of the public eye and because sages do not seek rewards or fame for what they do. As the *Wenzi* notes,

> As [Heaven] gives birth to beings, no one can see it nurturing, yet all beings grow ... sages emulate this: when they promote blessings, no one sees how they do it, yet blessings arise, and when they remove calamities, no one sees how it happens, yet calamities disappear.
>
> (Wenzi §12)

> [Sages] are not ostentatious when successful and not fearful when destitute. They do not show off when famous, and they are not ashamed to be unknown.
>
> (Wenzi §60)

In the same way that *Dao* is relatively obscure and somewhat hidden to most observers, sages similarly avoid trying to become famous. Unlike many insecure and attention-seeking people who are flowery in their speech and hypocritical in their actions,

> Sages inwardly cultivate the arts of the Way and do not put on an external show of humanitarianism and dutifulness. To know what is good for the senses and the body and roam in the harmony of the vital spirit is the roaming of the sage.
>
> (Wenzi §17)

> People in ancient times who sustained themselves took pleasure in virtue and did not mind lowliness, so reputation could not affect their will. They took pleasure in the Way and did not mind poverty, so profit could not move their minds. Therefore they were sober yet capable of enjoyment, quiet and able to be serene.
>
> (Wenzi §62)

> Those who are at peace ... do not want to be lustrous like jewels ... Animals with fine markings are stripped of their hides, those with beautiful horns are killed. Sweet springs are used up, straight trees are cut down ... mountains are torn up when their rocks contain jade.
>
> (Wenzi §45)

As seen in the passages above, there are a number of practical reasons why sages embrace an ethics of relative obscurity. Most obviously, relative obscurity contributes to one's safety and longevity by protecting one against resentment, retaliation, and revenge by those who dislike what you do or decide to target you because you are well-known and visible. By avoiding attacks against one's self that are motivated by others' resentment, the sage has a greater likelihood of achieving longevity which is naturally beneficial to the myriad creatures because it increases the amount of time sages are alive in this world to do good things and to serve as a model for others to follow.

Tranquility

A third ethical imperative of Daoist sages mentioned in the *Wenzi* is tranquility. Unlike ordinary men and women who are often impatient, frequently stressed, and typically dissatisfied with something or other in their lives, sages are perfectly at ease. Sages stay relaxed and enjoy an internal peace of mind. They are calm and not easily perturbed by things. As the *Wenzi* relates,

> Great people are peaceful and have no longings, they are calm and have no worries.
>
> (Wenzi §2)

Those who embody the Way do not become angry or overjoyed.

(Wenzi §43)

Real people ... they sleep without dreams and awake without worries.

(Wenzi §4)

[Sages] pass their lives in peaceful serenity and open calm, neither alienating anyone nor cleaving to anyone. Embracing virtue, they are warm and harmonious, thereby following Heaven, meeting with the Way, and being near to virtue. They do not start anything for profit or initiate anything that would cause harm.

(Wenzi §31)

In the *Wenzi*'s formulation, sages are "real people" (真人 *zhen ren*) also translatable as true/genuine/realized people who enjoy tranquility at all times. Their tranquility is so thorough they remain unshaken and unstirred even when a catastrophe or emergency arises.

When nothing can be done about something, enlightened people do not concern themselves with it.

(Wenzi §94)

To use a finite lifetime to worry and grieve over the chaos of the world is like weeping into a river to increase its water in fear of its drying up. Those who do not worry about the chaos of the world but enjoy order in their own bodies can be engaged in conversation about the Way.

(Wenzi §62)

If one lacks the arts of the Way to assess appropriate measure and wants, nobility and rank, then all the power and wealth in the world will not be sufficient to make one pleased and happy. So sages are even-minded and easygoing. Their vital spirits are guarded within, and cannot be deluded by things ... Sages do not want anything and do not avoid anything. When you want something, that may just make you lose it; and if you try to avoid something that may just bring it about.

(Wenzi §131)

As we see in these passages, in ordinary times sages experience deep peace, but even when facing obstacles, they still remain remarkably unperturbed. This is because sages are tightly connected to and firmly rooted in *Dao*. Hence, neither a gust of wind nor a ravishing cyclone can sway or uproot them. Because they are so well grounded, sages do not fluctuate between excitement and disappointment in response to the stimuli of life. Rather they stay focused and clear. As the *Wenzi* explains,

> When people become very angry, that destroys tranquility, when people become very joyful, that dashes positive action. Energy diminished, they become speechless. Startled and frightened, they go crazy. Anxiety and lament burn the heart, so sickness builds up. If people can get rid of all these, then they merge with spiritual light.
>
> (Wenzi §8)

Sincerity

A fourth ethical characteristic of the Daoist sage as described in the *Wenzi* involves what might be called sincerity and trustworthiness. This refers to being "uncontrived," meaning to live in a way that is full of genuineness and authenticity. It means not faking, not pretending, and being real and true to one's actual being, thoughts and feelings. Pursuing sincerity includes being open-minded to perceive the truth and pursuing genuine knowledge of the Way rather than having one's thoughts and perceptions about life be determined or overwhelmingly shaped by typical socialization processes. In the *Wenzi*'s view, to be sincere is to be without contrivance just like the Way:

> The great Way has no contrivance. Without contrivance, there is no possessiveness … it is imperative to keep to the great Way as the mother of the world.
>
> (Wenzi §23)

> Realize genuine knowledge, and don't use twisted reasoning. Keep yourself open, unminding, and you may attain clarity and all-around mastery. How could this be unknowing?
>
> (Wenzi §5)

> There is nothing that truth does not penetrate.
>
> (Wenzi §141)

> Real people … act without contrivance, work without striving, and know without intellectualizing.
>
> (Wenzi §4)

Correspondingly, the *Wenzi*'s ideal is for sincere, uncontrived sages to lead in governing the world to spread sincerity and knowledge of *Dao* to all of humanity. Other people are then likely to emulate sages and look up to them as moral exemplars. Through this process, the Daoist sage leaders' commitment to sincerity brings liberation to the people:

> It is simply that the leadership extends its sincerity throughout the world. Therefore to reward the good and punish the violent is correct order. What makes it operable is pure sincerity. Although directives may be clear, they cannot be carried alone, but must await pure sincerity. So if leadership is exercised over people but people do not follow, it is because pure sincerity is not there.
>
> (Wenzi §11)

> It is said, "When I contrive nothing, the people evolve on their own. When I strive at nothing, the people prosper on their own. When I enjoy tranquility, the people correct themselves. When I have no desires, the people are naturally plain."
>
> (Wenzi §7)

> The loftiest behavior in the world puts honesty and trust-worthiness above personal bonds.
>
> (Wenzi §85)

> Sages cultivate the basis within and do not adorn themselves outwardly with superficialities. They activate their vital spirit and lay to rest their learned opinions. Therefore they are open and uncontrived, yet there is nothing they do not do.
>
> (Wenzi §2)

As the *Wenzi* repeatedly emphasizes, sages are sincere and genuine. They do not just put on a show pretending to be virtuous. They are truly virtuous, and there is nothing contrived about them.

Meditation

In the *Wenzi*, we find that meditation forms an integral part of the Daoist sage's ethics and way of life. Meditation is a pathway to experiencing greater tranquility and sincerity in life and taking inspiration from *Dao* as discussed in Chapter 3. The sage takes refuge in meditation as a vital component of their spiritual cultivation. As the *Wenzi* describes it, meditation is a means for sages to regularly re-connect with *Dao*:

> Clarifying their eyes, they do not look, quieting their ears, they do not listen. Closing their mouths, they do not speak, letting their minds be, they do not think. Abandoning intellectualism, they return to utter simplicity,

resting their vital spirit, they detach from knowledge. Therefore they have no likes or dislikes. This is called great attainment.

(Wenzi §33)

As to the roaming of sages, they move in utter emptiness, let their minds meander in the great nothingness; they run beyond convention and go through where there is no gateway. They listen to the soundless and look at the formless; they are not constrained by society and not bound to its customs.

(Wenzi §18)

If there is nothing shrouding the spirit, and nothing burdening the mind, you are completely clear and thoroughly in tune, peaceful and unconcerned. Power and profit cannot tempt you, sound and form cannot seduce you, speechmakers cannot sway you, intellectuals cannot move you, warriors cannot frighten you. This is the freedom of real people.

(Wenzi §36)

Now if we would clarify a bowl of water, it takes at least a day before we can see our eyebrows and eyelashes reflect in it, but it only takes one shake to make it so turbid that we cannot see anything in it. Like a bowl of water, the vital spirit in human beings is hard to clarify and easy to muddle.

(Wenzi §37)

As discussed in multiple passages in the *Wenzi*, meditation is valuable because it leads us to become more humble and less interested in fame or reputation. It eliminates the distractions and ailments in our minds and therefore provides a freedom unparalleled by anything else in this world. However, stilling the mind and emptying one's thoughts is not easy. For most people, it takes considerable practice to still the mind, to "detach from knowledge," and to let the mind "meander in the great nothingness" (Wenzi §18).

Impartiality

A sixth characteristic of the Daoist sage's ethics in the *Wenzi* can be called impartiality. This principle is yet again a way of imitating and resembling *Dao*. It is based on a crucial recognition that *Dao* creates and nourishes all life and therefore has neither likes nor dislikes in the conventional sense. It does not mean that one should be indifferent. Rather, one should think, act, and love without prejudice or discrimination. *Dao* seemingly supports everyone's and everything's development without bias or favoritism as does the sage:

The Way of heaven has no personal preferences or personal rejection.

(Wenzi §13)

Universal benefit without discrimination is one with heaven and earth; this is called virtue ... If you are in a superior position, don't be proud of your success; if you are in a subordinate position, don't be ashamed of your problems. If you are wealthy, don't be arrogant; if you are poor, don't steal. Always keep impartial universal love and do not let it fade.

(Wenzi §74)

[To the sages ...] Nothing pleases them, nothing pains them, nothing delights them, and nothing angers them. All things are mysteriously the same, there is neither right nor wrong.

(Wenzi §4)

Mimicking *Dao*, the sage leads by impersonal mechanisms and institutions when governing so that no one is unfairly helped or harmed. As long as people do good, they are rewarded, and whenever they do bad, they are punished. The sage is not partial in such matters and is not swayed by personal considerations. When making decisions that will impact society, the sage does not unfairly treat his or her own friends, co-ethnics, schoolmates, or family members better than strangers. As the *Wenzi* notes,

To have trustworthy men distribute goods does not compare to determining portions and drawing lots. Why? Because the attitude of the concerned toward fairness is not comparable to that of those who are not concerned. To have honest men guard goods does not compare to shutting the doors and locking up completely, because the attitude of the desirous toward honesty is not comparable to that of those who have no desire.

(Wenzi §55)

The rewards and punishments dealt out by enlightened rulers are not for what people have done for the rulers themselves, but for what they have done for the country. To those who please the rulers themselves but do not do anything for the country, they do not give rewards; on those who offend the rulers themselves but are useful to the country, they do not visit punishments.

(Wenzi §109)

A balance is impartial; that is why it can be used for a scale. A plumb line is impartial; and that is why it can be used for a rule. The law of a true leader is impartial; that is why it can be used for direction. When there is neither favoritism nor hidden resentment, this is reliance on the Way and accord with human hearts.

(Wenzi §140)

In conducing public affairs, the sage is consistently opposed to corruption, bias, and prejudice in designing and implementing policies. The sage opts instead for impartiality in governing over clientelism, cronyism, nepotism, or favoritism. The *Wenzi* states:

> The way of human leaders does not involve contrivance, but it does involve following. It involves establishment, but it does not involve favoritism. When there is contrivance, there is argument; where there is favoritism, there is flattery. When there is argument, usurpation is possible; when there is flattery, seduction is possible.
>
> (Wenzi §150)

> If the rulers have no likes or dislikes, they are not resented for executions or blessed for charity. They follow standard guidelines without personal involvement in affairs, like sky and earth, covering and supporting all.
>
> (Wenzi §88)

Loving-kindness

In the *Wenzi*, one observes that Daoist sages are not the kind of people who are just interested in benefiting themselves. Rather, the sage is someone who is caring and loving in their thoughts and actions toward others. As the *Wenzi* asserts,

> "Disliking exclusivism and loving everyone" are mate of the world.
>
> (Wenzi §48)

> When sages govern people, they see to it that people suit their individual natures, are secure in their homes, live where they are comfortable, work at what they can do, manage what they can handle, and give their best. In this way all people are equal, with no way to overshadow each other.
>
> (Wenzi §120)

> If there is love for people, no one is punished because of a grudge.
>
> (Wenzi §103)

> When the rulers are wise, they guide and judge fairly; wise and good people are in office, skilled and capable people are at work. Wealth is distributed downward, and all the people are aware of their blessings.
>
> (Wenzi §174)

The *Wenzi* calls for practicing loving-kindness in one's thoughts and in one's actions. Sage-kings make sure people are safe and have food to eat. Sages are also mentally attuned to finding out what the common people need so those needs can be met:

> The mind of sages does not forget the desire to help others, day or night, and the extent to which its benefit reaches is far indeed.
>
> (Wenzi §29)

> [Sages] do not worry whether their own lives will be short, they worry about the hardships of the common people. Therefore they are always empty and uncontrived, embracing the elemental and seeing the basic, not getting mixed up in things.
>
> (Wenzi §124)

Emptiness/Simplicity

The ethical principle of emptiness and simplicity is fundamentally embodied by the Daoist sage. In the *Wenzi*, sageliness is characterized by letting go of unnecessary desires and relinquishing excesses in one's life and in one's mind. The key to achieving such simplicity is to be neither overly ambitious, nor to exhaust the body. This implies achieving a proper work-life balance in order to keep one's mind and body in a healthy condition. The *Wenzi* tells us,

> Unadulterated purity and plain simplicity are the trunk of the way. Emptiness means there is no burden within. Evenness means the mind is untrammeled. When habitual desires do not burden you, this is the consummation of emptiness.
>
> (Wenzi §3)

> Real people embody this through open emptiness, even easiness, clear cleanness, flexible yielding, unadulterated purity, and plain simplicity ... Their perfect virtue is the Way of heaven and earth, so they are called real people.
>
> (Wenzi §4)

> [Sages] do not dare to be excessive. They use nonbeing to respond to being and are sure to find out the reason, they use emptiness to receive fullness and are sure to find out the measure.
>
> (Wenzi §31)

Simplifying one's life is made possible by reducing the thoughts in one's mind and the demands on one's body. By doing so, sages are able to live moderately in a basic, pure, and simple way:

> Sages minimize their affairs, which are thus orderly. They seek to have little, and thus are sufficed.
>
> (Wenzi §19)

> Rank, power, and wealth are things people crave, but when compared to the body they are insignificant. Therefore sages eat enough to fill emptiness and maintain energy, and dress sufficiently to cover their bodies and keep out the cold. They adjust to their real conditions and refuse the rest, not craving gain and not accumulating much.
>
> (Wenzi §33)

> Sages are comfortable in poverty, enjoying the Way. They do not harm life by craving and do not burden themselves by materialism.
>
> (Wenzi §155)

> To govern the body and nurture essence, sleep and rest moderately, eat and drink appropriately; harmonize emotions, simplify activities. Those who are inwardly attentive to the self can attain this and are immune to perverse energies.
>
> (Wenzi §58)

As seen in the passages above, while sages may be content even when living in poverty, the overall message of the *Wenzi* does not advocate asceticism. In the *Wenzi*, simplicity just means not having too much and not being very materialistic. So, for instance, having 1.5 acres of land should be enough for a family. This implies that if a family owned five acres of land, then it would be ok if they were taxed at perhaps 20%–25% of their grain (so that others would also have food to eat), but it would be excessive to tax them very highly at say 75%–80%:

> Human life is such that if one man cultivates no more than an acre and a half and harvests no more than five hundred pounds of grain, then his family can eat … Enlightened leaders of ancient times limited what they took from their subjects and were moderate in their own living …. They shared the same pains and pleasures as the people, so there were no downcast people in all the land.
>
> (Wenzi §152)

> Those who are born into nobility become arrogant, those who are born into riches become extravagant. Therefore wealth and status are not conducive to understanding the Way.
>
> (Wenzi §155)

Discussion and Conclusion

As identified in this chapter, there are certain core ethical characteristics of the Daoist sage as found in the received text of the *Wenzi*. These ethical qualities include humility, relative obscurity, tranquility, sincerity, meditation, impartiality, loving-kindness, and emptiness/simplicity. These principles are mentioned multiple times throughout the text of the *Wenzi* and are closely in tune with characteristics of the "true" or "sacred" person as prescribed in a number of other Daoist classics.

Based on the foregoing analysis, there are several conclusions we can make about the ethics of the Daoist sage. Firstly, as the discussion above illustrates, the Daoist sage ideal as described in the *Wenzi* is neither a-ethical nor unethical. Clearly, there is an ethical disposition to the Daoist sage, and what distinguishes the Daoist sage from the Buddhist monk, the Confucian gentleman, or the Catholic priest among others is that the ethical considerations and priorities among these archetypes are not identical.

Secondly, I would like to clarify that I am not asserting here that the eight ethical principles mentioned above are the only qualities of a Daoist sage as depicted by the *Wenzi* nor am I making any claims about their rank order or prioritization – nor does the *Wenzi*. What we can say with confidence is that these eight ethical principles feature prominently in the *Wenzi*'s description of the Daoist sage and these principles are also found in Laozi's *Daodejing* and other Daoist classics as well.[5]

Thirdly, what unites the eight ethical characteristics of the *Wenzi*'s Daoist sage as detailed above is their connection to *Dao* (the Way). What the *Wenzi* relates is that sages deviate from the social norm, but they do so in a good way because they (alone) have mastered and retained the Way among humans. Sages are therefore especially important when it comes to governance. As the *Wenzi* tells us,

> When sages are in positions of leadership, the people are happy with their government, when sages are among the masses, people look up to their ideas. In their determination they do not forget the desire to help others.
>
> (Wenzi §26)

> Examples of losing the Way are extravagance, indulgence, complacency, pride, attention to the extraneous, self-display, self-glorification, competitiveness, forcefulness, making trouble, forming grudges, becoming commanders of armies, and becoming leaders of rebellions. When small people do these things, they personally suffer great calamities. When great people do these things, their countries perish. At best it affects the individual, in worse cases it affects generations to come; no crime is greater than lacking the Way.
>
> (Wenzi §72)

Fourthly, becoming a sage is not something that just happens to someone after they become a leader. Rather the causal sequence is the other way around. In the *Wenzi*, we find that "sagehood has nothing to do with governing others but is a matter of ordering oneself" (Wenzi §4). In fact, paradoxically, the *Wenzi* tells us that "to be able to rule the world, it is essential to have nothing to do with the world" (Wenzi §36). This means one needs to first and foremost be(come) a spiritual rather than a materialistic creature. As the *Wenzi* explains,

> The Great Way is even, and not far from oneself. Cultivate it in yourself, and that virtue is real. Cultivate it in others, and that virtue is endless.
>
> (Wenzi §95)

> If you have the Way, you guide people thereby; without the Way, you will be controlled by others.
>
> (Wenzi §158)

> All things can be overcome, except the Way, which cannot be overcome.
>
> (Wenzi §127)

As seen in these passages, sages overcome ethical deficits and failures in their own lives and get their own self in order before governing others. This refers to valuing and taking good care of the self that the *Dao* has given us, and it implies that political leaders must be a spiritual leader or at least spiritually fit. People become in tune with the Way when sages cultivate the Way in themselves first. Sages can then cultivate it in others by way of their mindset and behavior as a model.

To conclude, key ethical principles of the Daoist sage are spelled out in the text of the received *Wenzi*. These principles provide guidance not only for understanding a particular model of behavior that has been cherished and admired for over two millennia within the Daoist tradition but also for giving the modern day Daoist adept or aspirant a guide by which to live their lives.

Notes

1 In this article, I follow convention in referring to Wenzi as if he were the author of the text, while acknowledging that the mythical Wenzi as a historical disciple of Laozi probably never actually existed (Van Els 2014, 2018).

2 Considering these mixed origins, the received Wenzi has been categorized as a Daoist "patchwork text" drawing on "various sources, namely, the proto-*Wenzi*, the *Huainanzi*, the *Mengzi*, the *Guanzi*, and a few other texts" such as Laozi's *Daodejing* (Van Els 2018: 113).

3 The other three texts were the *Daodejing* (*Laozi*), *Zhuangzi*, and *Liezi*.

4 English translations of the *Wenzi* in this chapter are taken from Cleary (1992).

5 For a discussion of some of these principles in Laozi, see Joshi (2024c).

5   Toward a Sustainable Daoist Economy

Lessons from the *Daodejing*

In the 21st century, countries will need to rapidly reduce their environmental degradation and adopt better policies to mitigate climate change in order to enable humans and other species to survive into the future. But what kind of economic model represents a more sustainable alternative to the status quo? As examined in this chapter, the philosophy of sustainability expressed in the classical Daoist (a.k.a. Taoist) text of the *Daodejing* (DDJ) (a.k.a. *Tao Te Ching*) by Laozi (a.k.a. Lao-tzu) offers such an alternative. In particular, this chapter focuses on three core principles of the DDJ which guide us to embrace an economy that is (a) in harmony with nature, (b) synergistically satisfies human needs, and (c) is centered upon meaningful work involving worker autonomy, work-life balance, and optimal experience.

As a number of scholars have highlighted, classical Daoist thought generally favors ecological sustainability (e.g. Girardot, Miller and Liu 2001; Lai 2003; Rowe and Sellmann 2003; Chan 2009; Miller 2013a, 2013b, 2017; Xing and Starik 2017; Nelson 2020; Joshi 2022). Yet, there are conflicting interpretations over Daoist economic prescriptions (e.g. Dorn 1998; McCormick 1999; Moeller 2006; Barbalet 2011; Tang 2014; Behuniak 2015; Guo, Krempl and Marinova 2017). Some have argued that the Daoist economic ideal articulated by Laozi is a capitalist-oriented economy allowing profit-seeking non-state actors to act without restrictions in an economy that runs on its own without any (or with minimal) public management (e.g. Dorn 1998; McCormick 1999). Yet, others contend that the Daoist classics strongly repudiate a capitalist market economy (e.g. Moeller 2006; Graupe 2007; Behuniak 2015) with some believing that Daoist economic philosophy explicitly leans toward a socialist viewpoint permitting only public rather than private ownership of property (e.g. Tang 2014).

Addressing the question of how classical Daoist thought might be compatible with the imperative of a healthy and sustainable economy, this chapter begins by comparing different scholarly conceptions of Daoist economics. It then argues that the Daoist thought of Laozi's DDJ contains three key principles with major implications for sustainable economies. Firstly, Daoist economic thought emphasizes nourishing the lives of humans and other species

DOI: 10.4324/9781003517344-5

(*yangsheng* 養生) (see Chapter 2) and hence we should avoid negatively interfering with (i.e. not damage) the natural (i.e. non-human) world to the greatest extent possible. Secondly, Laozi's rejection of desire (*wuyu* 無欲) strongly implies that the global economy should follow a needs-based rather than a wants-based (demand-driven) system. This implies that a sustainable economy is one that satisfies people's fundamental human needs rather than permitting a few to accumulate great fortunes, dominate others, and be wasteful. Thirdly, Daoist economic thought with its emphasis on naturalness (*ziran* 自然) and spontaneous attunement (*wuwei* 無爲) (see Chapter 3) supports favorable labor conditions and meaningful work involving work-life balance, worker autonomy, and creativity. As the chapter concludes, Daoist economic thought provides useful guidelines for transitioning toward more sustainable and fulfilling economies.

Literature Review

A key idea in Daoist economic thought is the concept of *wuwei* which can be translated as a type of non-action, non-coercive action, or non-calculating action (e.g. Slingerland 2000). By contrast, the opposite of *wuwei* is "reckless, aggressive, and harmful actions toward self, society, and natural order" (Snyder 2006: 115; see also Liu 2001). As Zhang (2015: 216) asserts, "For Daoists, the conception of *wuwei* challenges any action that is coercive, purposive, and egocentric." There are, however, competing interpretations over the economic meaning of *wuwei*. Interpreting it as complete non-interference (by rulers or governments), Western anarchists have found in *wuwei* a justification for getting rid of the state, while Western libertarians find in *wuwei* a basis for adopting a *laissez-faire* economy based on the idea that "*laissez-faire* is simply an extension of *wu-wei* to government policy" (McCormick 1999: 334). For example, citing DDJ chapter 57, Dorn (1998: 4) argues that

> Rulers rule best when they rule least; that is, when they take "no unnatural action." … the foregoing passage implies that the more the state intervenes in everyday life, the more rent seeking and corruption there will be. Alternatively, if people are left alone to pursue their own happiness, a spontaneous market order will arise and allow people to create prosperity for themselves and their country.

Dorn supports combining the idea of "spontaneous market order" together with the "freedom of contract" and "well-defined private property rights" with the latter representing a significant form of state intervention in the natural order of things, but his overall argument is that less government ownership and fewer state-imposed restrictions on economic activity exemplify a Daoist economic position or what he labels "market Taoism" which calls for shrinking the size of the state and expanding the size of the market and civil society. As he states,

> The idea that people have a natural tendency to make themselves better off if left alone to pursue their own interests, and the notion that a laissez-faire system will be harmonious if government safeguards persons and property, are the foundation of the West's vision of a market-liberal order, but they are also inherent in the ancient Chinese Taoist vision of a self-regulating order – an order we might properly call "market Taoism."
>
> (Dorn 1998: 7)

However, Dorn's interpretation has been contested by many scholars. As Graupe (2007: 7, 8) asserts, the "market Taoism" position rests upon a false dichotomy that "if you are not in favor of the state you necessarily have to be in favor of the market," whereas Daoism actually favors "*neither* the state *nor* the market simply because it operates in an entirely different universe of discourse as *both* the theory of the market and the theory of the state." Furthermore, Graupe finds no evidence that "Daoists believe the pursuit of one's own (material) interests could automatically promote that of the society. On the contrary, in both the *Dao De Jing* and the *Chuang Tzu*, selfish behavior and endless desires are considered as the root causes of suffering" (ibid.: 9).

Similarly, Behuniak (2015) rejects the "market Taoism" interpretation on account of the importance of frugality, fairness, and reducing desires in Daoist thought. As he argues,

> In respect to economic concerns, the Daodejing is not so very different from other Chinese philosophical schools. We see the same general themes here as elsewhere: a distrust of the profit motive and concerns over vital industries, unfair taxation, and the misallocation of state treasure … But unlike other philosophers, Laozi did not wish to increase the size of the kingdom.
>
> (Behuniak 2015: 288)

As Behuniak concludes, "to neglect Daoism's teachings on the reduction of desire, and to altogether ignore its own economic ideal, results in an unacceptably truncated version of Daoism … The result is not Daoism" (ibid.: 293). Similarly, Barbalet (2011: 349) highlights how Daoist thought may be compatible with some aspects of a market economy, but at the same time its "containment of desire, the promotion of contentment and the notion that frugality generates riches all point in the direction of an egalitarian rather than an unequal economy."

Highlighting the importance of equality, Tang (2014: 121) further argues that the Daoist economy is fundamentally incompatible with capitalism because "Daoists argue against the private ownership system." Supporting his claim, Tang references DDJ chapter 51 which states that "people can produce things but should not appropriate them to themselves." In Tang's view, unlike Confucian ethics which focus on "serving the state's supreme interest," Daoist ethics are centered upon human development of the individual (ibid.). Thus, when following a Daoist approach, "both individuals' economic activities and national administration should comply with nature" (ibid.: 110). This means individuals should "'restrain from selfishness and desires' and 'avoid being harmed by material things' so as to achieve the greatest freedom of body and mind and natural longevity" (ibid.: 111). As Tang (2014: 132) notes, "Laozi believes that the natural law is to oppose any surplus" and the DDJ "advocated thrift and opposed extravagance" meaning that "Daoists seek to eliminate disparities of wealth between the rulers and the ruled" and they oppose "working for wealth for the ruling class" (ibid.: 125).

Other scholars have noted how Daoist thought emphasizes the cyclical nature of life (e.g. Ling 2014) implying support for a circular economy (e.g. Hennig 2017: 25). As Miller (2013b: 120) explains,

> If Daoist philosophy has anything to contribute to notions of development, it is from within this circular perspective, in which the functioning of a system is basically understood not as a simple linear growth but as continuous exchange. Translated to an economic sphere this invites a theory of development rooted not in Christian or post-Christian faith in continuous linear development towards some ever-unattainable utopian ideal, but rather a more realistic and holistic view that pays attention to the overall health and wellbeing of the community.

Similarly, Guo et al. (2017: 271) note how in the Daoist perspective, "humans are the children of nature who have to respect Heaven and Earth. Their actions or behaviors need to follow the natural rules (*Dao*)," but humans are also "allowed to improve the natural conditions because they are not passive."

As this review of the literature reveals, there are competing conceptions of Daoist economic thought. Nevertheless, most scholars reject the "market Taoism" interpretation while emphasizing the importance of reducing desires, avoiding surplus, and the supremacy of the natural world in Daoist thought. Building off these insights, I will now highlight three key principles in Daoist thought with major implications for sustainable economics. I will also discuss their overlaps with recent innovations and discoveries in the fields of community development, industrial ecology, and cognitive psychology.

Harmony with Nature

A first key principle of classical Daoist thought with major implications for sustainable economics is respect for and harmony with nature. This refers to humans letting all things live their natural life course and not causing them (either through actions or inactions) to die prematurely (Kohn 2012). In the Daoist worldview, health and longevity are "fundamental virtues" involving both "healing within the body (of the individual or the community) and also to defend the body from negative environmental factors" (Miller 2013b: 118). As Zhao (2016: 203) explains, "because of the equal importance of the physicality and spirituality in humanity and because of the fragile nature of the individual human life, one should always place health and longevity first." In particular, the Daoist idea of nurturing life (*yangsheng*) champions nourishing, preserving and cherishing one's own life and to the extent possible the life of other humans and species (including animals and plants). This has significant economic implications.

As Nelson (2020: 15) argues in his book on Daoist environmental philosophy, the Daoist ideal of *yangsheng* is one in which "the genuine sage-king rules for the sake of nourishing the life of the people and the myriad things, bringing benefit without contending and without seeking acknowledgement such that people to the maximal degree possible govern themselves." This approach is guided by the principle of "rejection of domination" (Xing and Starik 2017: 1305) whereby non-domination of nature can mean either leaving it alone or being in a cooperative relationship of stewardship (Snyder 2006: 121). As Schipper (2001: 82–83) highlights, 20 out of the "180 Precepts of Lord Lao," a classical Daoist text, relate to preserving the natural environment. Thus, respecting nature has long been important in Daoism. Moreover, according to the Daoist principle of *wuwei*, humans should generally refrain from disturbing nature and humans should allow nature to flourish on its own. This perspective naturally "disallows overly consumptive practice which is the chief contributor to the degradation of the natural environment ... from the Daoist perspective a virtuous person must also be an environmentally virtuous person" (Chan 2009: 143). As Nelson summarizes,

Early Daoism entails (1) non-harming and (2) nurturing and cherishing life of individual creatures in their plurality and collective species of creatures in their biodiversity as well as its interconnected self-reproducing relational systems ... Daoist discourses recommend caring, nourishing, and tending to – without the partiality of favoring some and discarding others – the life of things.

(Nelson 2020: 68)

To achieve this in practice requires "ecosystem sustainability" as "a precondition of the cultivation of virtue or human flourishing [that] presupposes physical conditions such as oxygen, water, food, and fiber that sustain the person as a living being over time" (Chan 2009: 135).

In the Daoist perspective, respect for nature stems from the belief that "human society is neither isolated from nor a privileged segment within nature.

The Daoist ruler's mandate is to minimize human aspirations to overstep the human mandate ... Any aspirations to impose a human rule over nature have to be prevented by the sage-ruler" (Moeller 2006: 66). In Laozi's view, nature is neither attention-seeking nor conceited. It just gets things done and moves on its way. Likewise, sages are neither pretentious nor covetous (see Chapter 4). As Laozi states,

> Sages desire to be without desires and show no regard for precious goods. They study what is not studied and return to what the multitude pass by. They work to support the myriad creatures in their natural condition.[1]
>
> (DDJ 64)

The sage's humility derives from a recognition that:

> Dao is the ultimate source and the fundamental governing principle of all things including nature. To put it differently, nature manifests the Dao. As for the human-nature relation, humans play a more humble role. Nature for human beings is not something that we can dominate or manipulate. Instead, nature is something that we have to learn from, that is, something like our teacher instead of our servant ... As the student-teacher relation is marked by respect, the Daoist conception of human-nature relation also requires us to show our respect to nature and to cultivate this disposition in ourselves.
>
> (Chan 2009: 142).

As for economic policy choices to support sustainability and the healthy living of all creatures, one of the most important is to prevent war and violence. As Laozi states,

> Weapons are inauspicious instruments. All creatures find them repulsive. And so one who has the Way does not rely upon them ... Peace and quiet are the highest ideals. A military victory is not a thing of beauty. To beautify victory is to delight in the slaughter of human beings. One who delights in the slaughter of human beings will not realize his ambitions in the world.
>
> (DDJ 31)

As the DDJ makes clear, "nothing is more catastrophic than war since it brings about killing, mutilation, and widespread devastation" (Zhang 2012: 479). Therefore, countries and their rulers ought to be content with their size even if they are small and seek to neither increase their territory nor the size of their army nor population numbers (Behuniak 2015: 291).

In addition to avoiding war, the Daoist priority of harmonizing with nature nudges us to pursue waste-free industrial ecology as seen in the example of eco-farming at Fiji's Montfort Boys' Town School where the five micro-industries of growing mushrooms, raising chickens and pigs, capturing methane gas for electricity, managing fish farms, and growing hydroponic plants have been linked together by "using the waste of one agricultural industry as fertilizer or fuel for another, in a loop that will dump little or no pollution into the environment" (Kane 1997: 28). In an integrated system like this, "it is the ecological need that selects which kinds of fish are raised, and which other crops are produced" and this differs significantly from an unmanaged market economy in which "the prices of fish and crops are set according to the tastes and demands of buyers" (ibid.: 31). An integrated and non-polluting system of eco-farming as seen in Kane's (1997) study of the Montfort Boys' Town School sustainably embodies the principle of *wuwei* as it involves no (or minimal) negative interference to the natural ecology and environment. Likewise, the production and consumption of local organic foods involve less interference and harm to nature compared to usage of non-organic industrial fertilizers, pesticides, herbicides, and genetically manipulated crops. To sum up, minimizing harm to natural biological and ecological processes and species is a key pillar of the Daoist *yangsheng* economy.

Needs-Based Economy

A second key principle of Daoist economic thought is humans meeting their basic needs. This implies that the global economy should follow a needs-based rather than a wants-based (demand-driven) model. What is important is for people to satisfy their fundamental human needs in a simple way and not for some people to accumulate great wealth or to dominate others. As Laozi states:

> Not paying honor to the worthy leads the people to avoid contention. Not showing reverence for precious goods leads them to not steal. Not making a display of what is desirable leads their hearts away from chaos. This is why sages bring things to order by opening people's hearts and filling their bellies. They weaken the people's commitments and strengthen their bones. They make sure that the people are without knowledge or desires. And that those with knowledge do not dare to act. Sages enact non-action and everything becomes well ordered.
>
> (DDJ 3)

As emphasized in the Laozi passage above, sage rulers of the state (or the world) should non-coercively achieve (a) opening of people's hearts, (b) filling of their bellies, (c) weakening of people's commitments, and (d) strengthening of their bones. Rulers should also (e) make people without distorted knowledge or desires, (f) not pay honor to the worthy, (g) not show reverence for precious goods, and (h) not make a display of what is desirable. Here being "without knowledge" as discussed in Chapter 3 does not refer to advocating ignorance but rather to not have any biases in how one interprets the world and to not be saturated by government propaganda or ideological indoctrination of any sort. This implies that the economic policies of enlightened sage rulers should softly lead people away from greed (weaken their desires), hunger (fill their bellies), illness (strengthen their bones), delusion (be without misleading knowledge), anger/hatred (open people's hearts), and frustration (weaken their clinging and attachments to things that are impermanent or illusory).

To meet these objectives, national governments, local governments, and international organizations would be expected to reform their education policies so as to help open people's hearts, reform their food policies to help fill people's bellies, reform their media policies to help weaken people's lust for luxuries, and reform their health policies to help strengthen the people's bones. As for making people "without knowledge" (i.e. not brainwashed) and without insatiable desires, governments would need to reform their media and education systems so that people are not saturated by one-sided propaganda. This implies allowing for pluralistic circulation of competing perspectives coupled together with restrictions against false claims and hate speech. It also implies putting some limits and/or restrictions on advertising (to not make a display of what is desirable), instituting reasonable salary caps, and placing limits on land/property holdings and annual bonuses (i.e. to not pay honor to the worthy) while deflating the value of scarce high-priced art works, antiques, gems, and collectibles (to not show reverence for precious goods).

Underlying this vision of a sustainable economy is the Daoist idea of reducing desires (*wuyu*) based on the principle that "excessive attention to desire led by sensation distracts from satisfaction of human needs" (Barbalet 2011: 348). By "getting rid of desire," Daoists refer especially to the "elimination of unwarranted and unnatural greed rather than desires that conform to people's natural needs" (Tang 2014: 117). As Laozi states,

> The greatest misfortune is not to know contentment. The worst calamity is the desire to acquire. And so those who know the contentment of contentment are always content.
>
> (DDJ 46)

> In bringing order to the people or in serving Heaven, nothing is as good as frugality.
>
> (DDJ 59)

The lesson here is that a sustainable economy should produce few (if any) luxury goods and most economic activity should be directed toward fulfilling people's nutritional, health, housing, and other needs. In order to promote sustainability, there should be little (or no) advertising promoting expensive and unnecessary luxury products as this may cause people to become envious and desirous of what they do not have (Moeller 2006: 91). As Moeller (2007: 110) explains, from the Daoist perspective, "the desire to acquire is the core reason for political unrest and the competition between countries or societies" and "there is no limit to the cycle of addiction that occurs in such states of desire. Only satisfaction that arises from the mastery of cessation can be lasting."

From the Daoist perspective, individuals and the economy as a whole should avoid (a) overspending, (b) overproducing, (c) overconsuming, and (d) hoarding. As Laozi asserts,

> Abandon profit and robbers and thieves will be no more ... Manifest plainness. Embrace simplicity. Do not think just of yourself. Make few your desires.
>
> (DDJ 19)

As Moeller (2007: 22) explains, "from a Daoist perspective the accumulation of goods and wealth will, paradoxically, lead to loss and perhaps disaster. The advice is therefore not to hoard things." This gets to the core of Laozi's position which rejects conspicuous consumption and instead promotes simplification and consuming only that which is essential. In Laozi's view,

> The five colors blind our eyes. The five notes deafen our ears. The five flavors deaden our palates. The chase and the hunt madden our hearts. Precious goods impede our activities. This is why sages are for the belly and not for the eye. And so they cast off the one and take up the other.
>
> (DDJ 12)

As seen here, the Daoist vision implies a needs-based economy where people's fundamental human needs are fulfilled. This differs significantly from a wants-based, demand-based, and desire-based economic system where some people have great material excess and surplus but still lack contentment while others remain in deficit unable to meet their basic human needs.

As for putting these ideas into practice, Laozi's emphasis on meeting people's needs closely resembles the "human scale development" (HSD) approach of Manfred Max-Neef (1992: 197), a barefoot economist who championed a relatively decentralized economy and politics based on "the satisfaction of fundamental human needs" combined with self-reliance and organic articulations from civil society. HSD calls for development on a small scale since "attaining the transformation of an object-person into a subject-person in the process of development is, among other things, a problem of scale" (ibid.: 198). The HSD approach is based on the principle that all humans need to satisfy the interrelated fundamental human needs of subsistence, protection, understanding, leisure, affection, participation, creation, identity, and free-dom. These are taken to be the needs of all people in all societies with there being no hierarchy among these needs except for subsistence which necessarily comes first. What differs across cultures in the HSD perspective is which satisfiers are employed to meet those needs with there being "no one-to-one correspondence between needs and satisfiers" (ibid.: 199). For instance, a satisfier of a specific need might turn out to be a violator or destroyer of meeting other fundamental needs or it may be a pseudo-satisfier, inhibiting satisfier, or singular satisfier. The optimal approach is therefore to pursue synergistic satisfiers which simultaneously satisfy multiple needs without inhibiting the satisfaction of any other needs.

As Max-Neef (1992: 205) argues, "synergistic satisfiers" are usually gen-erated endogenously by communities themselves at the grass roots level, whereas other less optimal satisfiers tend to be imposed upon people.[2] Simi-larly, Daoist classics emphasize people acting autonomously to find solutions to their own problems. They stress that humans have inherent inclinations but unfortunately are socialized to think and act in certain ways by the dictates of society and its rulers who often impose counter-productive systems and ideas on people that are at odds with what is best for individual humans. Thus, from a Daoist perspective, people reducing desires for unnecessary things, coming up with their own integrated and synergistic solutions to meeting their needs, and experiencing pure present contentment are essential to achieving sustain-able economies, peace, and happiness.

Valuable Work

As Max-Neef (1992: 202) has argued, closely resembling the critique of early Daoists, we find ourselves today in "an alienated society engaged in a pro-ductivity race … the question of the quality of life is overshadowed by our obsession to increase productivity." By contrast, the Daoist thought of Laozi and Zhuangzi supports the idea that humans should work to live rather than live to work and that our work should be meaningful in the sense of being both instrumentally and intrinsically rewarding. Thus, a third core principle in Daoist thought of relevance to sustainable economics is the value of labor and meaningful work as well as work-life balance, worker autonomy, and experiencing creativity/flow in work.

Underpinning the Daoist vision of labor is the concept of *wuwei* as men-tioned earlier. As Slingerland (2000: 300) notes, *wuwei* refers to

A state of personal harmony in which actions flow freely and instantly from one's spontaneous inclinations – without the need for extended deliberation or inner struggle – and yet nonetheless perfectly accord with the dictates of the situation at hand [to] display an almost supernatural efficacy …

Wuwei in the work place and in work activities involves displacing mindless behavior and ordinary, conventional knowledge/values in favor of labor that involves "a high degree of concentration on the part of the agent" and which "allows for a considerable amount of flexibility of response" (ibid.).

As Graupe (2007: 6) explains, in the Daoist view, labor and work should be "a *self-creative* and *co-creative* process, which functions at its best when freed of coercion and outside constraint." Thus, "rather than implying that people should adopt a *passive and receptive* approach to the social order, the *Dao* is to be understood as the creative 'letting-go' of any egotistic behavior ... creative and spontaneous change is not attributed to some outer force, but to the field of our own activities itself" (ibid.: 9). Truly acting creatively and spontaneously therefore requires us to "transcend all pre-given roles. In order to discover the secret of their craft, for example, Zhuangzi's artisans must leave behind all external and social pressures. [They] mentally free themselves to concentrate creatively on the skill of their craft. The orientation of the performance of the task transforms it from work to making art" (ibid.: 11).

In the same way that Daoism seeks to transform work into art, Daoist emphasis on *wuwei* in and at work has been theorized by modern psychologists via the concept of *flow* as a term representing "optimal experience" which generally involves the following:

First, the experience usually occurs when we confront tasks we have a chance of completing. Second, we must be able to concentrate on what we are doing. Third and fourth, the concentration is usually possible because the task undertaken has clear goals and provides immediate feedback. Fifth, one acts with a deep but effortless involvement that removes from awareness the worries and frustrations of everyday life. Sixth, enjoyable experiences allow people to exercise a sense of control over their actions. Seventh, concern for the self disappears ... Finally, the sense of the duration of time is altered; hours pass by in minutes, and minutes can stretch out to seem like hours. The combination of all these elements causes a sense of deep enjoyment.

(Csikzentmihalyi 1990: 49)

Such "deep but effortless involvement" embodies the Daoist idea of *wuwei* as "people become so involved in what they are doing that the activity becomes spontaneous, almost automatic; they stop being aware of themselves as separate from the actions they are performing" (ibid.: 53). This kind of experience brings heightened satisfaction as people engage in such activities "not with the expectation of some future benefit, but simply because the doing itself is the reward" (ibid.: 67).

Work that involves *wuwei* and is flow-centric implies a significant degree of worker autonomy as *flow* is much more likely to occur when individuals set their own goals. As Graupe (2007: 8) clarifies, Daoists "deny the legitimacy of *all* top-down and supervenient governance while favoring a bottom-up, emergent and undetermined approach to ruling in which people themselves define the terms of social order." In the Daoist perspective, people's freedom stems from "deciding creatively and spontaneously on the patterns of harmonious coexistence within each unique situation of human encounter" (ibid.).

Work-life balance is therefore important for people to have sufficient time to follow their inner nature and to follow *Dao* instead of always being occupied by work (whether it is for their own survival or to create surplus wealth for themselves or others). As Ivanhoe (1999) clarifies,

> The actions of the truly virtuous arise spontaneously from their nature. They are not so much their actions as they are the Dao acting through them ... When hungry they eat, when tired they rest. In spring they plant, in autumn they harvest. They move as their nature commands, in harmony with greater rhythms, and in so doing "nothing is left undone."
>
> (ibid.: 248–249)

Having ample time away from work is also of great importance in Daoist thought which maintains that reproduction and nurturing life should take precedence over the production of commodities because in Daoism, "the cosmos is conceived of in terms of biological reproduction and fertility; it is understood as an 'organic' process of life" (Moeller 2007: 120).

To sum up, in Daoist economic thought, work ought to be meaningful, creative, and involve worker autonomy and work-life balance. In Laozi's vision, when sages are in power, they are neither indifferent to employee well-being nor biased in favor of employers. Rather, Laozi calls for leaders to be kind-hearted to all, impartial, uncorrupted, and free from bias. This type of leader is motivated to design meaningful jobs with autonomy and work-life balance for all to enjoy creative and flow-conducive jobs. By expanding such an approach throughout the global economy, dead-end and alienating jobs can be eliminated. As Laozi tells us,

> Sages do not have constant hearts of their own. They take the people's hearts as their hearts. I am good to those who are good. I also am good to those who are not good ... Sages blend into the world and accord with the people's hearts.
>
> (DDJ 49)

Conclusion

This chapter examined three pillars of a sustainable Daoist *yangsheng* economy. As indicated above, Daoist thought stresses (a) meeting our needs (rather than our wants), (b) meaningful work (rather than meaningless work), and (c) respect toward nature (rather than domination over nature).

The Daoist perspective on sustainable economics explored here also overlaps with a number of intellectual discoveries and innovations in the 20th century. Firstly, Laozi's emphasis on a needs-based economy resembles Max-Neef's (1992) "human-scale development". Max-Neef's integrated approach to meeting multiple needs with synergistic satisfiers minimizes both transaction costs and opportunity costs reflecting the Daoist imperative of *wuwei*. Secondly, Daoist emphasis on creativity and meaning in work resembles the optimal/autotelic experience of *flow* explored by positive psychologist Mihalyi Csikzentmihalyi (1990). Thirdly, the Daoist focus on harmony with nature resembles circular economy thinking, industrial ecology, and eco-farming as seen in the example of Fiji's Montfort Boys' Town School (e.g. Kane 1997).

To conclude, as a holistic philosophy, the classical Daoist thought found in Laozi's *Daodejing* encourages us to step off the hedonic treadmill and eliminate our addictions to wealth, consumption, and all those things and activities that "never lead to actual fulfillment" (Moeller 2006: 94). In contrast to currently popular economic strategies centered upon technological optimism, managerialism, or *laissez-faire*, Daoist economics calls for living simply and fulfilling needs. Building on the three pillars of Daoist *yangsheng* economics discussed here, it is hoped that future studies will continue to examine further applications of Daoist economic thought to enhance well-being and sustainability in our world today and to foster happiness, longevity, and enlightenment.

Notes

1 English translations from Laozi's *Daodejing* (DDJ) in this chapter are from Ivanhoe (2003).
2 According to Max-Neef (1992: 201), "satisfiers may include, among other things, forms of organization, political structures, social practices, subjective conditions, values and norms, spaces, contexts, modes, types of behaviour and attitudes, all of which are in a permanent state of tension between consolidation and change."

References

Ai, Amy L. 2006. "Daoist Spirituality and Philosophy: Implications for Holistic Health, Aging, and Longevity." In Elizabeth Mackenzie and Birgit Rakel, eds. *Complementary and Alternative Medicine for Adults: A Guide to Holistic Approaches to Healthy Aging*. New York: Springer, pp. 149–160.

Ames, Roger. 2011. "Introduction." In Ronnie Littlejohn and Jeffrey Dippmann, eds. *Riding the Wind with Liezi: New Perspectives on the Daoist Classic*. Albany: State University of New York Press, pp. 1–11.

Appel, Lawrence J. 2008. "Dietary Patterns and Longevity: Expanding the Blue Zones." *Circulation* 118(3): 214–215.

Arthur, Shawn. 2009. "Eating Your Way to Immortality: Early Daoist Self-Cultivation Diets." *Journal of Daoist Studies* 2(1): 32–63.

Arthur, Shawn. 2013. *Early Daoist Dietary Practices: Examining Ways to Health and Longevity*. Lanham, MD: Rowman and Littlefield.

Barbalet, Jack. 2011. "Market Relations as Wuwei: Daoist Concepts in Analysis of China's Post-1978 Market Economy." *Asian Studies Review* 35(3): 335–354.

Behuniak, James, Jr. 2015. "Two Challenges to Market Daoism." In Roger Ames and Peter Hershock, eds. *Value and Values: Economics and Justice in an Age of Global Interdependence*. Honolulu: University of Hawaii Press, pp. 283–295.

Bloch, Hélène. 2019. "From Daoist Cultivation to Longevity Market? 'Nourishing Life' on Mount Qingcheng." *Journal of Daoist Studies* 12(1): 163–80.

Blofeld, John. 1978. *Taoism: The Road to Immortality*. Boston: Shambhala.

Brindley, Erica. 2022. "Deconstructing 'Hedonism': Understanding Yang Zhu in the *Liezi*." In Carine Defoort and Ting-mien Lee, eds. *The Many Lives of Yang Zhu: A Historical Overview*. Albany: State University of New York Press, pp. 105–131.

Buettner, Dan. 2012. *The Blue Zones: 9 Lessons for Living Longer from the People Who've Lived the Longest*, 2nd Edition. Washington, DC: National Geographic.

Buettner, Dan, and Sam Skemp. 2016. "Blue Zones: Lessons from the World's Longest Lived." *American Journal of Lifestyle Medicine* 10(5): 318–321.

Cao, Feng. 2019. "Yang Zhu Research in the Twentieth Century: With a Focus on Guo Moruo, Meng Wentong, Hou Wailu, and Liu Zehua." *Contemporary Chinese Thought* 50(3–4): 144–163.

Carter, Eric D. 2015. "Making the Blue Zones: Neoliberalism and Nudges in Public Health Promotion." *Social Science and Medicine* 133: 374–382.

Chan, Jonathan. 2009. "Ecosystem Sustainability: A Daoist Perspective." In King-Tak Ip, ed. *Environmental Ethics: Intercultural Perspectives*. Leiden: Brill, pp. 133–143.

Chen, Shaoming. 2010. "On Pleasure: A Reflection on Happiness from the Confucian and Daoist Perspectives." *Frontiers of Philosophy in China* 5(2): 179–195.

Chen, Shaoming. 2019. "A Secondary Figure in the 'World of Classics': An Analysis of Yang Zhu's Image." *Contemporary Chinese Thought* 50(3–4): 92–103.

Chen, Yin-Ching. 2012. "The Idea of Nature in the Daoist Classic of Liezi." Ph.D. Dissertation, University of Illinois at Urbana-Champaign.

Chiang, Sing-chen Lydia. 2009. "Visions of Happiness: Daoist Utopias and Grotto Paradises in Early and Medieval Chinese Tales." *Utopian Studies* 20(1): 97–120.

Cleary, Thomas (trans.). 1992. *Wen-tzu: Understanding the Mysteries (Further Teachings of Lao-tzu)*. Boston: Shambhala.

Cohen, Elliot. 2009. "Psychology and Daoism: Resisting Psychologization—Assisting Dialogue." *Journal of Daoist Studies* 3(3): 151–162.

Coutinho, Steve. 2014. *An Introduction to Daoist Philosophies*. New York: Columbia University Press.

Csikzentmihalyi, Mihalyi. 1990. *Flow: The Psychology of Optimal Experience*. New York: Harper Collins.

Culham, Tom, and Jing Lin. 2020. *Daoist Cultivation of Qi and Virtue for Life, Wisdom, and Learning*. Cham: Palgrave Macmillan.

Daniels, Joel. 2019. "Uncarved and Unconcerned: Zhuangzian Contentment in an Age of Happiness." *Dao* 18(4): 577–596.

Davis, Donald D. 2011. "Daoism and Positive Psychology: Healing Self, Healing Society." In Livia Kohn, ed. *Living Authentically: Daoist Contributions to Modern Psychology*. Dunedin, FL: Three Pines Press, pp. 158–175.

Davis, Donald D. 2018. "Meditation, Taijiquan and Qigong: Evidence for Their Impact on Health and Longevity." *Journal of Daoist Studies* 11(1): 207–230.

Dear, David. 2012. "Chinese Yangsheng: Self-help and Self-image." *Asian Medicine* 7(1): 1–33.

Defoort, Carine. 2020. "Five Visions of Yang Zhu Before He Became a Philosopher." *Asian Studies* 8(2): 235–256.

Defoort, Carine, and Ting-mien Lee, eds. 2022. *The Many Lives of Yang Zhu: A Historical Overview*. Albany: State University of New York Press.

Dorn, James A. 1998. "China's Future: Market Socialism or Market Taoism?" *CATO Journal* 18(1): 131–146.

Emerson, John. 1996. "Yang Chu's Discovery of the Body." *Philosophy East and West* 46(4): 533–566.

Engelhardt, Ute. 2000. "Longevity Techniques and Chinese Medicine." In Livia Kohn, ed. *Daoism Handbook*. Leiden: Brill, pp. 74–108.

Fech, Andrej. 2015. "The Protagonists of the Wenzi in Light of Newly Discovered Materials." *Oriens Extremus* 54: 209–248.

Fox, Alan. 2008. "Guarding What Is Essential: Critiques of Material Culture in Thoreau and Yang Zhu." *Philosophy East and West* 58(3): 358–371.

Franceschi, Claudio, and Massimiliano Bonafè. 2003. "Centenarians as a Model for Healthy Aging." *Biochemical Society Transactions* 31(2): 457–461.

Fung, Yu-Lan. 1983. *A History of Chinese Philosophy, Vol. I*. (trans. Derk Bodde). Princeton: Princeton University Press.

Girardot, N.J., James Miller, and Liu Xiaogan, eds. 2001. *Daoism and Ecology: Ways within a Cosmic Landscape*. Cambridge, MA: Harvard University Press.

Graham, A. C. (trans.). 1990. *The Book of Lieh-tzu: A Classic of Tao*. New York: Columbia University Press.

Graham, A. C. (trans.). 2001. *Chuang-Tzu: The Inner Chapters*. Indianapolis: Hackett.

Graham, A. C. 1989. *Disputers of the Tao: Philosophical Argument in Ancient China*. Chicago: Open Court.

Graupe, Silja. 2007. "Do Daoist Principles Justify Laissez Faire Policies? A Critical Examination of 'Market Daoism." *International Journal for Field-Being* 6(1): 1–16.

Guo, Xiumei, Sandra Krempl, and Dora Marinova. 2017. "Economic Prosperity and Sustainability in China: Seeking Wisdom from Confucianism and Taoism." In Lech W. Zacher, ed. *Technology, Society and Sustainability: Selected Concepts, Issues and Cases*. Cham: Springer, pp. 263–273.

Hansen, Chad. 1992. *A Daoist Theory of Chinese Thought: A Philosophical Interpretation*. New York: Oxford University Press.

Haybron, Daniel M. 2013. *Happiness: A Very Short Introduction*. New York: Oxford University Press.

He, Aiguo. 2019. "From 'Beast' to 'Philosopher of Rights': On the Newly Shaped Modern Structure of Yangism." *Contemporary Chinese Thought* 50(3–4): 104–118.

Hennig, Alicia. 2017. "Daoism in Management." *Philosophy of Management* 16(2): 161–182.

Hitchcott, Paul Kenneth, Maria Chiara Fastame, and Maria Pietronilla Penna. 2018. "More to Blue Zones than Long Life: Positive Psychological Characteristics." *Health, Risk & Society* 20(3–4): 163–181.

Hoff, Benjamin. 2019/1982. *The Tao of Pooh and the Te of Piglet*. London: Farshore.

Huta, Veronika. 2013. "Eudaimonia." In Susan A. David, Ilona Boniwell, and Amanda Conley Ayers, eds. *The Oxford Handbook of Happiness*. New York: Oxford University Press, pp. 201–213.

Ivanhoe, Philip J. (trans.). 2003. *The Daodejing of Laozi: Translation and Commentary*. New York: Seven Bridges Press.

Ivanhoe, Philip J. 1999. "The Concept of *De* ('Virtue') in the Laozi." In Mark Csikszentmihalyi and Philip Ivanhoe, eds. *Religious and Philosophical Aspects of the Laozi*. Albany: State University of New York Press, pp. 239–257.

Ivanhoe, Philip J. 2011. "The Theme of Unselfconsciousness in the *Liezi*." In Ronnie Littlejohn and Jeffrey Dippmann, eds. *Riding the Wind with Liezi: New Perspectives on the Daoist Classic*. Albany: State University of New York Press, pp. 127–149.

Ivanhoe, Philip J. 2013. "Happiness in Early Chinese Thought." In Susan A. David, Ilona Boniwell, and Amanda Conley Ayers, eds. *The Oxford Handbook of Happiness*. New York: Oxford University Press, pp. 263–278.

Izutsu, Toshihiko. 1984. *Sufism and Taoism: A Comparative Study of Key Philosophical Concepts*. Berkeley: University of California Press.

Joshanloo, Mohsen. 2014. "Eastern Conceptualizations of Happiness: Fundamental Differences with Western Views." *Journal of Happiness Studies* 15(2): 475–493.

Joshi, Devin. 2012. "Does China's Recent 'Harmonious Society' Discourse Reflect a Shift towards Human Development?" *Journal of Political Ideologies* 17(2): 169–187.

Joshi, Devin. 2020. "The Other China Model: Daoism, Pluralism, and Political Liberalism." *Polity* 52(4): 551–583.

Joshi, Devin. 2021. "The Way of Longevity: Blue Zones as Unselfconscious Models of Daoist Living." *Journal of Daoist Studies* 14(1): 128–151.

Joshi, Devin. 2022. "Daoist Political Ecology as Green Party Ideology: The Case of the Swedish Greens." *Nature and Culture* 17(3): 288–313.

Joshi, Devin. 2023. "Daoist Feminist Leadership for International Peace: The Case of Jeanette Rankin." *International Feminist Journal of Politics* 25(2): 179–200.

Joshi, Devin. 2024a. "An Integrated Theory of Happiness: The Yang Zhu Chapter of the *Liezi*." *Journal of Daoist Studies* 17(1): 1–25.

Joshi, Devin. 2024b. "From *Guo* to *Tianxia*: Linking Two Daoist Theories of International Relations." *International Relations of the Asia-Pacific* 24(1): 1–27.

Joshi, Devin. 2024c. "A Daoist Political Leadership Approach to Nonviolence: The Case of Olof Palme." *Journal of Pacifism and Nonviolence* 2(1): 122–150.

Kahneman, Daniel. 2012. *Thinking, Fast and Slow*. New York: Penguin.

Kane, Hal. 1997. "Eco-Farming in Fiji." *World Watch* 10: 28–34.

Kohn, Livia. 2009. "Told You So: Extreme Longevity and Daoist Realization." In Calvin Mercer and Derek Maher, eds. *Religion and the Implications of Radical Life Extension*. New York: Palgrave Macmillan, pp. 85–96.

Kohn, Livia. 2010. *Daoist Dietetics: Food for Immortality*. Dunedin, FL: Three Pines Press.

Kohn, Livia, ed. 2011. *Living Authentically: Daoist Contributions to Modern Psychology*. Dunedin, FL: Three Pines Press.

Kohn, Livia. 2012. *A Source Book in Chinese Longevity*. St. Petersburg, FL: Three Pines Press.

Kushner, Thomasine. 1980. "Yang Chu: Ethical Egoist in Ancient China." *Journal of Chinese Philosophy* 7(4): 319–325.

Li, Jinglin. 2010. "Mencius' Refutation of Yang Zhu and Mozi and the Theoretical Implication of Confucian Benevolence and Love." *Frontiers of Philosophy in China* 5(2): 155–178.

Li, Yucheng. 2019. "The Emergence and Evolution of Yang Zhu as a 'Heretic' Symbol." *Contemporary Chinese Thought* 50(3–4): 119–132.

Ling, L.H.M. 2014. *The Dao of World Politics: Towards a Post-Westphalian, Worldist International Relations*. New York: Routledge.

Liu, Xiaogan. 2001. "Non-Action and the Environment Today: A Conceptual and Applied Study of Laozi's Philosophy." In N.J. Girardot, James Miller, and Liu Xiaogan, eds. *Daoism and Ecology: Ways within a Cosmic Landscape*. Cambridge, MA: Harvard University Press, pp. 315–340.

Liu, Xiaogan. 2011. "Daoism: Laozi and Zhuangzi." In Jay L. Garfield and William Edelglass, eds. *The Oxford Handbook of World Philosophy*. New York: Oxford University Press, pp. 47–57.

Liu, Gusheng, and Haijie Li. 2019. "The Thought of Yang Zhu in the History of Laozi's Thought: Along with a Discussion of the Authenticity of the Liezi." *Contemporary Chinese Thought* 50(3–4): 75–91.

Lobel, Diana. 2017. *Philosophies of Happiness: A Comparative Introduction to the Flourishing Life*. New York: Columbia University Press.

Max-Neef, Manfred. 1992. "Development and Human Needs." In Paul Ekins and Manfred Max-Neef, eds. *Real-life Economics: Understanding Wealth Creation*. New York: Routledge, pp. 197–213.

McCormick, Ken. 1999. "The Tao of Laissez-Faire." *Eastern Economic Journal* 25(3): 331–341.

Michael, Thomas. 2015. "Hermits, Mountains, and Yangsheng in Early Daoism: Perspectives from the Zhuangzi." In Livia Kohn, ed. *New Visions of the Zhuangzi*. St. Petersburg, FL: Three Pines Press, pp. 149–164.

Miller, James. 2013a. "Is Green the New Red? The Role of Religion in Creating a Sustainable China." *Nature and Culture* 8(3): 249–264.

Miller, James. 2013b. "Daoism and Development." In Matthew Clarke, ed. *Handbook of Research on Development and Religion*. Cheltenham, UK: Edward Elgar, pp. 113–123.

Miller, James. 2017. *China's Green Religion: Daoism and the Quest for a Sustainable Future*. New York: Columbia University Press.

Moeller, Hans-Georg. 2006. *The Philosophy of the Daodejing*. New York: Columbia University Press.

Moeller, Hans-Georg. 2007. *Dao De Jing (Laozi): A Complete Translation and Commentary*. Chicago: Open Court.

Nelson, Eric S. 2020. *Daoism and Environmental Philosophy: Nourishing Life*. New York: Routledge.

Phan, Chánh Công. 2007. "The Laozi Code." *Dao* 6(3): 239–262.

Poulain, Michel, Anne Herm, and Gianni Pes. 2013. "The Blue Zones: Areas of Exceptional Longevity around the World." *Vienna Yearbook of Population Research* 11: 87–108.

Rowe, Sharon, and James D. Sellmann. 2003. "An Uncommon Alliance: Ecofeminism and Classical Daoist Philosophy." *Environmental Ethics* 25(2): 129–148.

Sakade, Yoshinobu. 2008. "Wenzi." In Fabrizio Pregadio, ed. *The Encyclopedia of Taoism, Vol. II.*, London: Routledge, pp. 1041–1042.

Schipper, Kristofer. 2001. "Daoist Ecology: The Inner Transformation. A Study of the Precepts of the Early Daoist Ecclesia." In N.J. Girardot, James Miller, and Liu Xiaogan, eds. *Daoism and Ecology: Ways within a Cosmic Landscape*. Cambridge, MA: Harvard University Press, pp. 79–94.

Schwartz, Benjamin. 1985. *The World of Thought in Ancient China*. Cambridge, MA: Harvard University Press.

Seo, June Won. 2015. "The Liezi and Daoism." In Xiaogan Liu, ed. *Dao Companion to Daoist Philosophy*. Dordrecht: Springer, pp. 449–467.

Slingerland, Edward. 2000. "Effortless Action: The Chinese Spiritual Ideal of Wu-wei." *Journal of the American Academy of Religion* 68: 293–328.

Slingerland, Edward. 2014. *Trying Not to Try: Ancient China, Modern Science, and the Power of Spontaneity*. New York: Broadway Books.

Snyder, Samuel. 2006. "Chinese Traditions and Ecology: Survey Article." *Worldviews: Global Religions, Culture, and Ecology* 10(1): 100–134.

Sterckx, Roel. 2019. *Chinese Thought from Confucius to Cook Ding*. London: Pelican.

Stewart, Frances. 2014. "Against Happiness: A Critical Appraisal of the Use of Measures of Happiness for Evaluating Progress in Development." *Journal of Human Development and Capabilities* 15(4): 293–307.

Tang, Renwu. 2014. "A Comparison between Confucian and Daoist Economic Philosophies in the Pre-Qin Era." In Cheng Lin, Terry Peach, and Wang Fang, eds. *The History of Ancient Chinese Economic Thought*. New York: Routledge, pp. 106–139.

Tiwald, Justin. 2016. "Well-being and Daoism." In Guy Fletcher, ed. *The Routledge Handbook of Philosophy of Well-Being*. London: Routledge, pp. 56–69.

Tolle, Eckhart. 2004/1999. *The Power of Now: A Guide to Spiritual Enlightenment*. Vancouver: Namaste Publishing.

Tolle, Eckhart. 2005. *A New Earth: Awakening to Your Life's Purpose*. New York: Plume.

Tov, William, and Evelyn W.M. Au. 2013. "Comparing Well-being across Nations: Conceptual and Empirical Issues." In Susan A. David, Ilona Boniwell, and Amanda Conley Ayers, eds. *The Oxford Handbook of Happiness*. New York: Oxford University Press, pp. 448–464.

Van Els, Paul. 2014. "The Philosophy of the Proto-Wenzi." In Xiaogan Liu, ed. *Dao Companion to Daoist Philosophy*. Dordrecht: Springer, pp. 325–340.

Van Els, Paul. 2018. *The Wenzi: Creativity and Intertextuality in Early Chinese Philosophy*. Leiden: Brill.

Van Norden, Bryan. 2011. *Introduction to Classical Chinese Philosophy*. Indianapolis: Hackett Publishing.

Villaver, Ranie. 2015. "Does Guiji Mean Egoism? Yang Zhu's Conception of Self." *Asian Philosophy* 25(2): 216–223.

Wang, Robin R. 2012. *Yinyang: The Way of Heaven and Earth in Chinese Thought and Culture*. New York: Cambridge University Press.

Wang, Zhongjiang. 2015. *Daoism Excavated: Cosmos and Humanity in Early Manuscripts* (trans. Livia Kohn). St. Petersburg, FL: Three Pines Press.

Wang, Xiaoyang, and Bao Yan. 2017. "Ways to Immortality: In Popular and Daoist Tales." *Journal of Daoist Studies* 10(1): 149–56.

Watson, Burton. 1968. *The Complete Works of Chuang Tzu*. New York: Columbia University Press.

Watts, Alan. 1975. *Tao: The Watercourse Way*. New York: Pantheon.

Wei, Yixia. 2019. "Yang Zhu in the Eyes of Kang Youwei." *Contemporary Chinese Thought* 50(3–4): 133–143.

Wilber, Ken. 2000. *A Theory of Everything: An Integral Vision for Business, Politics, Science and Spirituality*. Boston: Shambhala.

Wong, Eva. 1997. *The Shambhala Guide to Taoism*. Boston: Shambhala.

Xing, Yijun, and Mark Starik. 2017. "Taoist Leadership and Employee Green Behaviour: A Cultural and Philosophical Microfoundation of Sustainability." *Journal of Organizational Behaviour* 38(9): 1302–1319.

Zhang, Ellen. 2012. "Weapons Are Nothing but Ominous Instruments: The Daodejing's View on War and Peace." *Journal of Religious Ethics* 40(3): 473–502.

Zhang, Ellen. 2015. "*Zheng* (征) as *Zheng* (正)? Daoist Challenge to Punitive Expeditions." In Ping-Cheung Lo and Sumner B. Twiss, eds. *Chinese Just War Ethics: Origin, Development, and Dissent*. London: Routledge, pp. 209–225.

Zhang, Ellen. 2019. "Forgetfulness and Flow: 'Happiness' in Zhuangzi's Daoism." *Science, Religion and Culture* 6(1): 77–84.

Zhang, Ellen. 2020. "Critique and Subversion: Rethinking Yang Zhu's Conception of 'Self.'" In Moeller Hans-Georg and K. Whitehead Andrew, eds. *Critique, Subversion, and Chinese Philosophy: Sociopolitical, Conceptual, and Methodological Challenges*. New York: Bloomsbury Academic, pp. 139–151.

Zhao, Yanxia. 2014. "Yang Zhu's 'Guiji' Yangsheng and Its Modern Relevance." *Philosophy Study* 4(3): 173–188.

Zhao, Yanxia. 2015. "The Spirit of Charity and Compassion in Daoist Religion." *Sociology and Anthropology* 3(2): 122–135.

Zhao, Yanxia. 2016. "Daoist Longevity and the Aging Society." *Journal of Daoist Studies* 9(1): 194–209.

Zhao, Yanxia. 2022. "Happiness and Well-Being from a Daoist Perspective." In Sugirtharajah Sharada, ed. *Religious and Non-Religious Perspectives on Happiness and Well-Being*. London: Routledge, pp. 130–148.

Index

sageliness 67
Schipper, Kristofer 75
self-appraisal 11
self-consciousness 39
self-creative process 81
sexual intimacy 33n26
sheng ren 41
simplicity 67–68
sincerity 62–63
Slingerland, Edward 80
social conformity 4
social interactions 21
societies 7, 8, 11–13, 23–25, 53, 55, 56, 64, 65, 72, 73, 80
spiritual enlightenment 34
spiritual practices 51
state of mind 40, 45
state of "no-mind" 48
surrender 50
surrendered action 50
sustainable Daoist economy 71–83; harmony with nature 74–77; literature review 72–74; needs-based economy 77–80; valuable work 80–82
synergistic satisfiers 80

taijiquan 50
Tang, Renwu 73, 74
thinking 36
tian li 39
Tolle, Eckhart 34–36; consciousness and enlightenment, perception 43–53; distorted knowledge, abandoning 47–49; not acting independently, source 49–51; oneness 43–44; prisoners of ego, humans 44–47; reuniting with source, enlightenment 51–53
Tongxuan Zhenjing 56
tranquility 60–62

true freedom 41
trustworthiness 62, 63
Tse, Lao 44
Tuanmu Shu of Wei 10

unhappiness 7
universalistic egoism 3

valuable work 80–82
Van Els, Paul 56
Villaver, Ranie 3
virtuous person 75
vital spirits 61

Warring States period 1
well-being 1, 11, 53
Wenzi 55–70
women 19, 47, 60
Wong, Eva 24, 33n20
worker autonomy 71, 72, 80, 82
work-life balance 67, 71, 72, 80, 82
wuwei 28, 49, 50, 72, 75, 77, 80–82

Xiang, Guo 4

Yangism 5, 17n27
yangsheng 8, 30, 47, 75
yangsheng economy 77, 83
Yang Zhu (Yangzi) 1–17; causal thinking 12; cherishing oneself 4–5; legendary figure of 2–5; preference hierarchy 9; textual sources 3–4
yin-yang balance 23

Zhang, Ellen Y. 3, 72
Zhao, Yanxia 5, 8, 11, 13, 20, 75
Zhuangzi 2, 4, 34, 38–40, 42, 47–49, 52, 55, 80, 81
ziran 41, 72

Printed and bound by CPI Group (UK) Ltd, Croydon, CR0 4YY

16/10/2024

01775115-0001